WOOD MACHINING

*A complete guide to effective and
safe working practices*

WOOD MACHINING

A Complete Guide to Effective and Safe Working Practices

NIGEL S. VOISEY

Fully illustrated

STOBART & SON LTD

LONDON

British Library Cataloguing in Publication Data
Voisey, Nigel S.
  Wood machining: a complete guide to
  effective and safe working practices.
  1. Woodworking machinery——safety measures
  I. Title
  621.9   TS850

  ISBN 0–85442–032–0

Published 1987 by Stobart & Son Ltd, 67–73 Worship Street, London, EC2A 2EL
Printed in Great Britain by A. Wheaton & Co. Ltd., Exeter

Contents

Introduction

The type of accident in which an operator is simply careless and follows a workpiece into a cutter with his hand is predictable but extremely difficult to guard against. The working part of a cutter must necessarily be exposed in order for the cutter to work at all. Of course, this category of accident should never occur if concentration is maintained. A first rule should therefore be: CONCENTRATE ON WHAT YOU ARE DOING.

Most accidents, however, do not occur as a direct result of carelessness, but through a lack of understanding of machine cutter dynamics. A workpiece can be picked up by a cutter during feed and thrown back at the operator with almost explosive force. Material rejecton, or "kick-back" as this is called, is the root cause of the majority of accidents in machine woodworking, either through the material itself hitting the operator or hands dropping onto suddenly exposed cutters. Obviously, an understanding of the forces encountered in machine feeding is an important first step in making safe, enjoyable and productive use of the machinery at your disposal. Armed with this awareness it should be possible to approach *any* woodworking machine with confidence and work out a system of operation that *guarantees* your safety.

The TEN GENERAL RULES explained in the following chapter are applicable to the operation of all hand-fed machines. Specific additional points relating to operator safety when using certain types of machine are covered in the chapters dealing with those machines.

Recognizing that small workshops may be equipped with machinery having guard systems which would not comply with current legislation and that they may also be used for operations forbidden under the Health and Safety regulations, it is essential that the *reasons* for their formulation be understood. This should in no way be construed as a suggestion that such machines be used in an unacceptably guarded state or that potentially hazardous operations be carried out. Rather, the operator should be competent to recognize the cutting and rejection forces likely to be encountered in any operation and adopt practices which ensure total control. Many guards, for example, are not simply provided to deflect machine waste or prevent careless contact with rotating cutters. They often play a vital role in preventing or limiting the effects of 'kick-back'.

For clarity, some line drawings and photographs do not show the necessary guards in position. The illustration at the beginning of each specific machine section however does show these guards and their purposes are explained in the text. If effective guards are not provided with your machine, they should be made up from suitable materials before putting such a machine to use.

Used with understanding, machinery will replace the need for the years of experience needed to achieve similar results by hand methods. It will also give the small workshop owner a real opportunity to compete successfuly with larger scale producers who can rarely work economically on "one-off" and small batch runs.

This book has been written to be readable rather than as simply a dry relation of legal requirements. I have therefore extracted much of the information that could be classified as "general practice" and that which would otherwise be repeated in each chapter and included those points and principles in Chapter One (TEN GENERAL RULES FOR SAFE MACHINE WOODWORKING), Chapter Ten (GENERAL HEALTH & SAFETY) and Chapter Eleven (WASTE EXTRACTION).

A reader seeking information on a specific machine such as the circular saw, spindle moulder, etc. should therefore read the chapter on that machine *in conjunction with* the three chapters mentioned above covering the broader aspects of that machine's use.

Ten General Rules for Safe Machine Woodworking

1. Work Must Always Be Fed Against The Direction Of Cutter Rotation.

There are no exceptions to this rule in hand-fed machining operations.

The cutting and feeding forces must always oppose each other at the point of contact (Fig. 1). If material is fed onto a cutter *with* its direction of rotation, the cutter will be pulling the work into itself and it will be found extremely difficult to control the feed. The predictable result is that the work will be snatched away from the operator. This occurrence happens so quickly that fingers may well be pulled across suddenly exposed cutters.

SAW BENCH

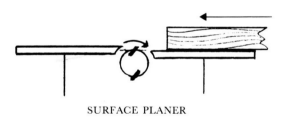

SURFACE PLANER

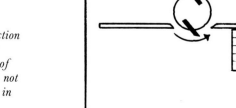

SPINDLE MOULDER (PLAN VIEW)

*Fig. 1 Feed must always be **against** the direction of cutter rotation. Withdrawal of a workpiece from a cutter is safe **only** if the precise line of original feed is maintained and the cutter does not make positive contact with a workface moving in the direction of cutter rotation.*

Withdrawal from long cuts on the saw bench, for example, should therefore be avoided.

In controlled feeding operations (i.e., *against* the direction of cutter rotation), the cutters will already have machined away any material on which they could pick-up if feed is stopped or the work withdrawn. (Fig. 2.)

NOTE: Withdrawing from a cut is safe *only* if the original line of feed is maintained. Cutters must not be allowed to make contact with any face moving in their direction of rotation.

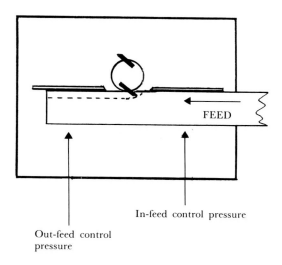

Out-feed control pressure

In-feed control pressure

FEED

Occasions When The First Rule Might Inadvertently Be Broken

a) BLIND CUTTING (DEEPING) ON THE SAW BENCH. In any sawing operation where the blade does not enter the work from above the incapacity of the tool to clear waste may result in the work riding up on the blade and leaving the feed support/ control surface. Reduced feed speed or increased location pressure from the operator may cause the work to "drop-on" to the blade with considerable risk of a kick-back. For this reason a circular saw should not be used for "blind" cutting which necessarily involves the additional risk of removing the saw guard and possibly the riving knife. *If the operator chooses to use the saw in this way, then great care must be taken to feed the work slowly in order that the cutting tips can clear the waste. In addition, adequate location pressure must be applied – preferably with a spring guard.* (Fig. 3).

b) "DROPPING ON" TO A ROTATING CUTTER. Machining cuts which are required to stop short of workpiece ends (stopped rebates, chamfers, moulds etc.) will have to be commenced by "dropping-on" to a rotating cutter. The operator must never

Fig. 2 The dotted line shows material machined away from the underside of the workpiece. Withdrawal from this cut is safe only if the cutter is not allowed to touch any part of the workpiece. In addition to downward control pressure which keeps the workpiece in firm contact with the machine table, pressure must be directed through the workpiece onto the control fences. This prevents either the nose or tail end of the work dipping into the cutter aperture.

(Spring type guards supplied with most spindle moulders should have a horizontal pressure shoe wide enough to direct pressure as shown and should overlap the aperture by at least 25mm (1") on either side).

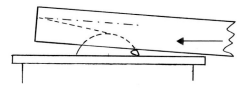

Fig. 3(a) – · – · – Intended line of cut. --------- Actual line of blind cut showing how workpiece has ridden up on the sawblade due to the reduced ability of the teeth to clear waste.

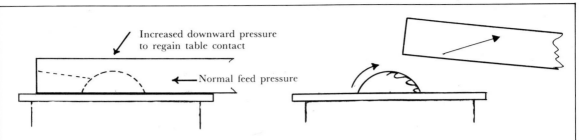

Fig. 3(b) Realization that the workpiece is "floating" on the blade (or cutter) will prompt increased downward control pressure to regain firm contact with the table. Cutter and work contact area is suddenly increased with consequent kick-back of work in the direction of cutter rotation.

Fig. 3(c) With the work kicked even slightly in the direction of cutter rotation the ascending rear teeth of the blade will be working into unmachined timber and the initial kick may be accelerated into total rejection of the workpiece.

attempt to control the considerable rejection forces encountered in this operation by hand restraint alone. A work-stop must be firmly clamped at the in-feed end of the table and work must be positioned against the stop before it is hinged onto the cutter. If the work is allowed to move even fractionally *with* the direction of cutter rotation, it may be accelerated to the full cutter peripheral speed (between 90–120 m.p.h.) in a fraction of a second. (Fig. 4.)

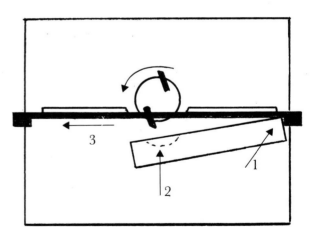

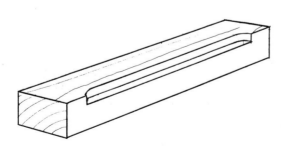

Fig. 4(a) "Stopped" mouldings are produced by "dropping-on" to a cutter.

Great care must be taken and proper procedures adopted to prevent any possibility of the work being kicked in the direction of cutter rotation.

Fig. 4(b) A through-fence has been superimposed and clamped or bolted to the split fences. The new fence incorporates stops at either end. Even if a complete through-fence is not used, a positively clamped stop MUST be used at the in-feed side of the cutter and the work located against the stop (1) before it is pivoted onto the cutter (2) and normal feed is commenced (3).

c) IMPROPER LOCATION OF WORK AGAINST CONTROL SURFACES. If work is prevented from making firm contact with feed support surfaces, say, through the interference of waste chips from previous machining, the work may roll off the interfering particles as the feed progresses bringing the rearmost part of the cutter into sudden contact with uncut material. The unexpectedly increased cutter force may prevent the operator from maintaining forward feed control and a kick-back will result. (Fig. 5.)

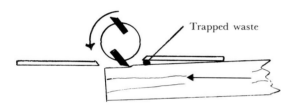

Fig. 5(a) Waste material may prevent proper location of the workpiece against guide fences or machine table.

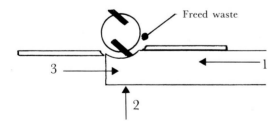

Fig. 5(b) As feed progresses (I), trapped waste may be carried along and freed allowing sudden relocation of the workpiece against the fence (2). This sudden increase in cutter/work contact area and the fact that the cutter can continue to work into unmachined material after the initial kick-back may result in total material rejection (3).

2. Work Must Always Be Of A Size Large Enough To Be Held Securely During The Entire Feed And Take-Off Operation.

Machine cutters have a relatively flat area of contact with workpieces when compared with the knife-edged presentation of most hand-held tools. Each time a machine cutter makes contact with the work a small shock is imparted and the workpiece must have sufficient mass or inertia to absorb this rejection force. The operator should feel no vibration or hammering through the body of the work being fed. Minimum size of material which can safely be fed will depend to a large extent on the sharpness of the cutters and the quantity of waste being machined away. In *every* case, the workpiece must be large enough to be held securely with both hands – not just the fingertips – and it should always be possible to complete the feed without the necessity of one or both hands passing directly over an unguarded cutter aperture.

As a general rule small components, such as the small moulded fillet in Fig. 6, should only be produced as an offcut from a larger workpiece which can be held securely.

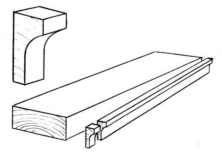

Fig. 6 First produce the moulded profile required on the edge of a wider board. Separate the moulded edge to the width required by rip sawing. Finally cut the fillets from the strip moulding in successive crosscuts.

Where the actual material to be machined is only available in unacceptably small or thin sections (exotic timbers, for example), it should be glued to a larger stabilizing block or so fed that its effective mass is increased by close contact with a feeding block or work-holding jig. (Fig. 7). (For moulding small workpieces with a vertical spindle moulder all the points mentioned above should be borne in mind *and* the additional protection of a through-fence should be considered essential – see Chapter 4.)

A major proportion of accidents, particularly in non-professional workshops, are traceable to attempts to machine work which cannot be held securely.

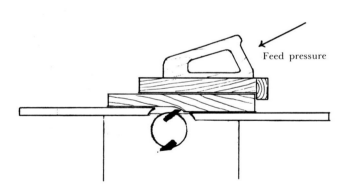

Feed pressure

Fig. 7 In some circumstances a push block can be used to increase the effective mass of small workpieces and guard the operator against the dangerously close proximity of fingers to rotating cutters otherwise unavoidable when manually feeding.

__Note__: Whether a push block is used or not, the workpiece must always be __at least__ four times the length of the cutter aperture so that adequate control surface (table/fence) contact is maintained at all stages of the feed. Waste material should also be machined away in a succession of light cuts rather than in a single pass.

3. Use The Appropriate Cutting Tool For Any Job At Its Optimum Speed

Machine tools rely on their own velocity, or the velocity of the work being fed to them, to cut efficiently. In fact, if the peripheral speed of a rotating cutter is reduced below a certain limit the cutting edges will not be capable of entering the work at all. In these circumstances the face of the cutter meets the work and can only reject it – often with considerable force. It is therefore important not to overload cutters by feeding at a rate too fast for the power available or the tool's waste clearance capabilities. The operator should aim to feed work at a speed which will allow the cutter to maintain revolutions near its free-running optimum.

For the same reason, undersized tooling fitted to a single speed machine may fail to achieve the peripheral speed necessary for it to work efficiently, thereby increasing the danger of hammering and kick-back. Single speed circular saws, for example, should display a warning notice specifying the minimum diameter of blade which can safely be fitted. This will be 60 per cent of the original blade diameter, assuming that the original blade was the largest that could properly be used. In other words, a saw bench fitted with a 250 mm (10″) blade by the manufacturers will have a shaft speed calculated to drive the periphery of the blade at approximately 3,000 metres (10,000 feet approx.) per minute. The smallest blade that can be substituted for the 250 mm (10″) original will be 60 per cent of that diameter, i.e. 150 mm (6″).

A further factor determining maximum feed speed before power demand exceeds power available will be the choice of cutter. In general, those cutters with widely pitched teeth will enable faster feed speeds to be utilized and deeper cuts to be taken than would be feasible with a similar tool having cutting tips set closer together. Firstly, there are fewer points of contact with the work face, and secondly, the increased gullet area (that is the space in front of the cutting tip), will allow a greater volume of waste to be carried through the body of the work until it can be discharged by centrifugal force as the tip leaves the work. Finely pitched cutters obviously have a smaller gullet and on deep or heavy cuts accumulated waste will block or interfere with the cutting ability of the tip. (Fig. 8.)

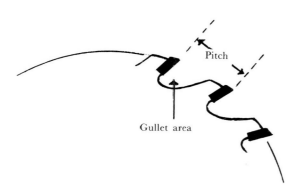

Fig. 8 "Pitch" is the term used to describe the distance between successive cutting teeth or tips. In the case of circular sawblades this is generally a broad descriptive term: "Coarse pitch" meaning wide tooth spacing and "fine pitch" meaning close tooth spacing. In the case of saw band blades the tooth pitch is specifically described in the number of teeth per inch. (t.p.i.).

The "gullet" is the space in front of each tooth or tip where sawdust accumulates while that tooth is buried in the work.

4. Plan All Machining Operations So That Feed & Take-off Areas Are Clear of Obstruction And Necessary Feeding Devices Are To Hand <u>Before</u> Starting A Cut.

In small workshops it will often be necessary to reposition machines to facilitate the handling of long or wide workpieces. Finding the exit path of a workpiece blocked once machining has commenced puts the operator in a dangerous position. He may be tempted to hold the work with one hand and stretch to move the obstruction so that the cut can be completed. He may attempt to withdraw from the cut, which can be equally dangerous if the precise line of original feed is not maintained. On the other hand, *stopping* the forward progress of a cut for any length of time is also very inadvisable as all working cutters depend on more or less continual progression into fresh material for cooling. In the case of a circular saw, the heat build-up in the plate can lead to critical plate distortion. (Power router users will know how quickly work heats to charring point if cut progression is stopped with the cutter in the work.) THERE IS NO SAFE OR RECOMMENDED WAY OF OVERCOMING THIS DIFFICULTY. Machining operations must therefore be *planned* to avoid it. If a workpiece is 2 metres (6 ft.) long, you will need at least the same length of clearance in front of, and behind, the machine head being used, and this must be ascertained before the operation is commenced.

Also included in pre-cut planning must be the provision of a suitable feeding device (i.e. a push-stick or block) where you know that a hand would otherwise have to pass dangerously close to any cutter. It is good workshop practice to have such feeding devices permanently sited with the machines where they are likely to be needed. You are then much less likely to "take a chance" when machining small quantities of work, and when the time and effort necessary to make such a safeguard seems out of proportion to the value of the job in hand. (Fig. 9.)

It should always be possible to complete any cut with a smooth and progressive feeding action. The operator's concentration and physical balance must never be adversely affected by lack of forethought and planning.

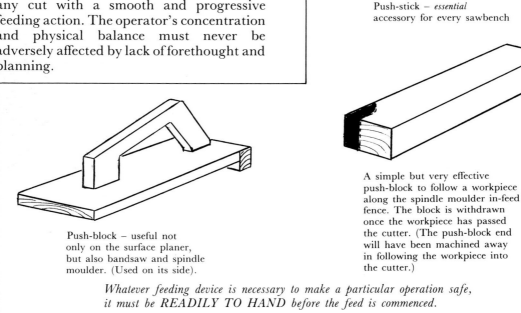

Fig. 9

Push-stick – *essential* accessory for every sawbench

A simple but very effective push-block to follow a workpiece along the spindle moulder in-feed fence. The block is withdrawn once the workpiece has passed the cutter. (The push-block end will have been machined away in following the workpiece into the cutter.)

Push-block – useful not only on the surface planer, but also bandsaw and spindle moulder. (Used on its side).

Whatever feeding device is necessary to make a particular operation safe, it must be READILY TO HAND before the feed is commenced.

5. Check That A Cutter Rotates Freely And That Guards/Movable Control Surfaces Are Securely Set Before Commencing A Cut.

Accidents frequently occur because operators forget to observe these simple procedures. A chuck key or shaft locking tool left in place after tool changing or guard adjustment can do considerable damage if the machine is switched on. When *any* adjustment has been made to a machine before or between successive machining operations, it is *essential* that cutter clearance and guard/fence security are checked. In

the case of a spindle moulder, for example, cutter projection is determined and set by moving and locking the fence/guard assembly. If this assembly moves during a cut due to increased control pressure and inadequate guard clamping, the effective cutter projection will be increased without warning to a point where material rejection or break-up will suddenly occur.

Always check, therefore, that a cutting tool will rotate freely through its full 360 degree cycle *and* that all relevant guards, fences, stops etc. are firmly clamped before putting a machine to use.

Guard and fence adjustments should be made with the machine switched off. Cutter changes or adjustments should be made with the power disconnected.

6. Use Work Supports In Any Operation Where You Would Otherwise Have To Move Around A Machine During The Progress Of A Feed/Take-off Operation.

In no circumstances during a hand-fed machining operation should it be necessary for the operator to move from the feed to the take-off side of a machine. Unless adequate support for work at the take-off (or out-feed) side of the machine is provided, however, such movement may be unavoidable. A roller support or frame is therefore essential for the support of long or heavy workpieces if adequate control is to be maintained without substantially varying table/fence control pressure. If the weight or overhang of out-fed material causes the work to leave the

Fig. 11 An adjustable roller support used to support work on out-feed from a spindle moulder. Lighter weight roller stands could be set in a concrete plinth for added stability. (Photo: Courtesy L.R. Flacke & Co., Cardiff.)

control surfaces a potentially dangerous situation has *certainly* arisen. The operator's hands may be brought into contact with the cutters, or, through suddenly increased cutter contact (e.g., "top-cutting" spindle operations – see Chapter 4), the work may break up or be rejected.

In all hand-fed machining operations it should therefore be possible to commence and complete the entire procedure from the in-feed side of the machine with no significant variation in the manual feed and control pressures applied.

In the small workshop an independent, variable height roller support will be found most useful for providing this essential support. Most roller supports of this pattern are of fairly light construction and additional ballasting (weighting) for added stability is advisable.

Fig. 10 This roller take off stand features a head that can be swivelled through 90° to provide either conventional work support in the direct line of feed or a roller track to give lateral support to work overhanging the side of the machine. (Photo: Courtesy Luna Tools & Machinery Ltd., Milton Keynes)

15

7. Do Not Attempt To Use Machines For Work Beyond Their "Common-sense" Capabilities.

The theoretical cutting capacity of any machine should not necessarily be regarded as its safe *practical* working capacity. Factors such as machine stability, work table/fence support areas, etc. must be considered – especially when machining long, wide or heavy workpieces. Simply because a circular saw has a blade projection of say 75 mm (3″), it should not be assumed that it is a suitable machine for cutting large sheet materials which may in fact be only 12 mm ($\frac{1}{2}$″) in thickness or less. The weight and size of the material may create a dangerous instability in the machine, the operator or both.

Determining where this limit lies is very much a matter of common sense, but certainly, if any workpiece is of such dimensions that the operator's concentration and physical efforts are largely occupied with supporting the work rather than feeding it, the operation should not be attempted. Stock materials should be converted to comfortably manageable sizes with hand or portable power tools *before* offering them to any standing machine.

When using any unfamiliar machine it is also a sensible procedure to become acquainted with its performance capabilities through progressive, *light* cutting operations. In this way you will develop a feel for safe feed rate limits in relation to power available and volume of stock removed.

8. Check For Material Defects.

Workpieces which are split may break up during machining, causing the main body of the work to lose contact with the control surfaces and, in so doing, the operator may be in considerable danger from flying debris or suddenly varying cutter force. Similarly, loose or dead knots on board edges should be removed before the edge is machined. Even though the knot may seem firm, it may be freed as the cutter relieves surrounding material and be thrown back at the operator.

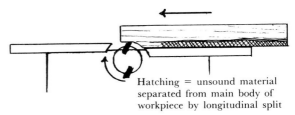

Hatching = unsound material separated from main body of workpiece by longitudinal split

Fig. 12 In any machine cut running into unsound material there is a danger that an unsupported section of the workpiece will be freed from the main body as sound timber is machined away. The freed section may then be rejected or broken up by the cutters with the added hazard of a "drop-on" of the main workpiece to the cutter.

Many thousands of eye injuries are reported in the woodworking industry every year and most are caused by chips or splinters being picked-up and rejected by cutters. It is therefore good practice to stand slightly to one side of the direct line of feed and not to look directly into any potential rejection path – even though work may not be being fed at that moment. This type of injury is very common on thicknessing units when the operator is tempted to peer into the in-feed aperture. Because of this it is also an excellent idea to wear some form of eye protection whenever machining operations are taking place. (See Chapter 10.)

9. Control Waste.

Many serious but totally avoidable accidents occur because waste chippings and work offcuts are allowed to accumulate around machines and on machine tables. The floor area in the vicinity of every machine in use

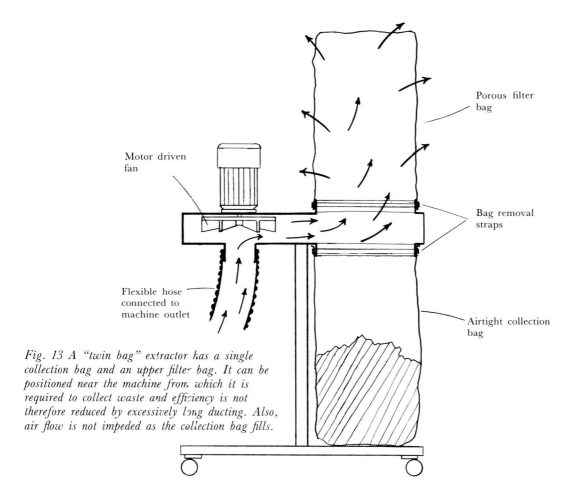

Motor driven fan

Porous filter bag

Bag removal straps

Flexible hose connected to machine outlet

Airtight collection bag

Fig. 13 A "twin bag" extractor has a single collection bag and an upper filter bag. It can be positioned near the machine from which it is required to collect waste and efficiency is not therefore reduced by excessively long ducting. Also, air flow is not impeded as the collection bag fills.

should be kept clear of anything over which the operator might stumble during the progress of a feed. Work tables should be free from waste which may prevent firm location of work to feed control surfaces and which may also be nudged into contact with rotating cutters. (Tools, cutting lists and all other non-essential materials should also be removed from the machine table before a cut is commenced.) An accumulation of waste inside cutter housings will also adversely affect cutter performance as waste particles will be picked up and carried around by the cutter to be impacted against the surface being machined.

Note: Never clear waste by hand from the immediate vicinity of rotating cutters – switch off.

This applies to the clearance of waste from all machines, including those such as the planer/thicknesser where waste builds up on the thicknessing bed during surface planing and it is common to see operators pushing it through the unit with a stick while the machine is still running. By the nature of the operation you will have to be looking into the thicknessing feed aperture and there is a real danger of the stick making accidental contact with the rotating cutter block.

Waste extraction systems are the most practical way of dealing with the problem and are considered essential for virtually all machines situated in a "factory" environment. For a small workshop, a mobile extractor, which can be connected to the waste outlet of various machines, will be found extremely useful. The "twin bag" type with upper filter and lower collection bags retains maximum efficiency until the collection bag is full and hood adaptors can easily be made for interchangeable connection if they are not already provided. An extractor will certainly make the workshop a much pleasanter place to use and benefits to general health are also notable as the fine-particle dust produced in the machining of many materials can be harmful.

Finally, dust in the vicinity of electrical switchgear can be a fire hazard and should be kept to a minimum. (Every workshop should be equipped with fire extinguishers suitable for use on electrically started fires and mounted at easily accessible points. See also Chapter 11.)

10. Check That Cutting Tools Are Sound And Properly Sharpened.

Blunt tools place an increased demand on power and transmission components and will tend to reject work due to their "hammering" rather than clean cutting action. An efficient cutting edge must therefore be maintained either through honing or re-grinding as appropriate.

All machine cutting tools need working clearance for the cutting edge. In other words, it is only the cutting edge itself which should be making contact with the work face and no part of the body of the tool or the roots of cutting tips should be in contact with the work. (Details of the few exceptions to this general rule will be found under specific machine headings.) Clearance angles are incorporated by relieving or grinding away the supporting part of a cutting tip or edge. In use, it will be found that clearance angles are affected by wear on the cutting edge itself, or, by a build-up of resin deposits on the relieved faces of the edge. Such deposits should be removed periodically by cleaning with a suitable solvent. (Cellulose thinners or oven cleaning fluid will be found very effective but the cutting tool should be removed from the machine before cleaning.) (Fig. 14.)

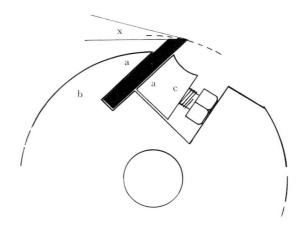

Fig. 14 Typical cutter block and cutter locking assembly. (one cutter only shown)

x: Clearance or "relief" angles may be affected by a build up of resin deposits. Clean with solvent.

a: Cutter may be improperly clamped due to dust etc. on seat/clamping block faces. Clean when changing cutters.

b: Area of potential weakness through severe overtightening of clamping bolt/"crash" stress. Check for cracks.

c: Threads on clamping bolts and in clamping blocks must be in good condition. Replace if worn or damaged.

Of course the *storage* of inflammable materials must be taken account of in dealing with general workshop safety and this is further explained in Chapter 10.

Apart from attention to cutting edges, the supporting body of the tool itself should be checked for soundness. A saw plate, for example, may develop cracks. It should "ring true" when removed from the machine and tapped. It may have lost "tension" (see Chapter 2) and "throw" or wander in a cut.

Other cutting tools such as planer knives or spindle moulder cutters rely on bolt locking or wedge compression for security. Bolts incorporated for this purpose *should* be of high-tensile material, but, particularly in the case of low-cost tools, this may not be the case and wear will occur which prevents adequate clamping of the cutters. Such components of a tool assembly should obviously be replaced. The use of cutter retention systems which incorporate *positive interlocking* between the tool body and the knife or cutter is increasingly favoured although not necessarily required by law. As the risk of a cutter leaving the tool body is practically eliminated by adoption of this construction it should be the operator's first choice where a choice exists. (See also Chapter 4.)

It is especially important to check the soundness of any tool which has been overloaded and jammed during feed. The forces it has been subjected to are considerable and may be in excess of the tool's design capabilities to withstand without damage. (Brazed-tip tools in particular, may suffer if they have come into contact with a workpiece at less than the peripheral speed essential for them to cut efficiently, and the joint between the tip section and the tool body may be fractured. Brazing may also be overheated and tips loosened during inexpert re-grinding. The servicing of cutting tools should, therefore, always be carried out by properly trained, conscientious personnel.)

*   *   *

Finally, these general operating procedures may be summed-up with this advice: Use machines within their practical capabilities (comon sense); work with materials that can be held securely; and, *plan* your cutting operations to take account of the entire feed and take-off procedures *before* commencing a cut.

Understanding the nature of machine cutting tools is a useful first step in making application of the rules automatically – rather like driving on the correct side of the road.

CHAPTER TWO

The Circular Saw Bench

In the small workshop the sawbench will be found a most useful machine for general conversion of timber and sheet materials. It should be appreciated, however, that the cut surfaces will almost always require further finishing in the case of face timbers or edges. With this in mind, *efficiency* in cutting, rather than perfection, is a more realistic aim. In theory, a fine-pitch blade will give a better finish than one with fewer teeth, but the cut is still unlikely to be of a standard that would make planing, thicknessing and sanding unnecessary, and the increased power demand when feeding a fine-pitch blade will necessitate slower feed speeds and will limit the bench's capabilities when deep cutting operations are called for.

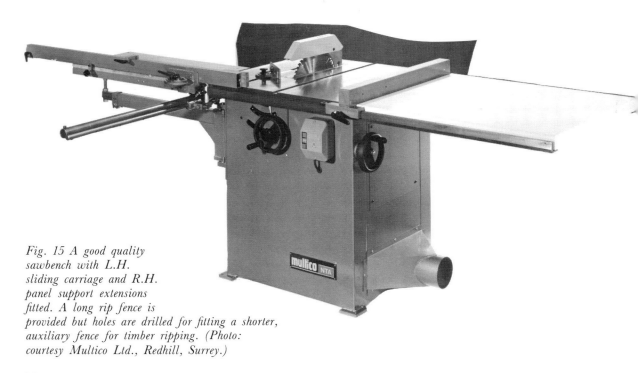

Fig. 15 A good quality sawbench with L.H. sliding carriage and R.H. panel support extensions fitted. A long rip fence is provided but holes are drilled for fitting a shorter, auxiliary fence for timber ripping. (Photo: courtesy Multico Ltd., Redhill, Surrey.)

Fig. 16

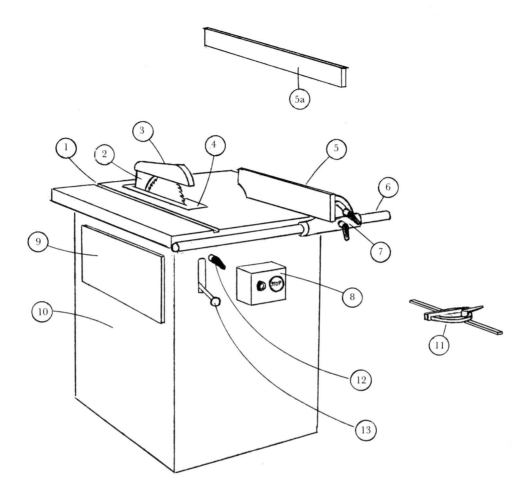

1 Table groove for protractor mitre fence
2 Riving knife
3 Crown guard (also called; top guard, saw guard and working guard)
4 Table insert – removeable (also called; aperture insert)
5 Rip fence
5a Long rip or panel fence (as alternative to 5)
6 Fence bar

7 Fence tilt and slide mechanisms
8 ON/OFF switch (also push button starter)
9 Access cover (must be fixed whilst saw is connected to mains power)
10 Cabinet (must completely shroud all under table moving parts)
11 Sliding protractor (or mitre) fence
12 Blade height lock
13 Blade rise & fall control

If workshop output is mainly centred around the conversion of thin, delicate or brittle materials, then there is obviously a good case for using a special-purpose blade. Such a blade will, however, be unsuitable for most other jobs and the operational down-time necessitated by frequent blade changing for various cuts will be an annoyance. Where single, independent machines are likely to be needed for general use, it is always a good idea to find a compromise solution to tooling or cutter requirements.

In the case of a sawbench, choice between steel or tungsten tipped saw blades is the first consideration. Tungsten Carbide Tipped (T.C.T.) blades will give at least one hundred times the life of steel equivalents between services and they are the only blades suitable for the conversion of man-made, resin-bonded and coated boards. Also, because cutting tip "clearance" is achieved without the alternate lateral "set" of conventional steel blade teeth, T.C.T. blades will give a much more acceptable finish, even when a coarse pitch rip blade is used for cross-cutting or for sheet material conversion. My choice of a single blade for general use is, therefore, a T.C.T. *rip blade*, which will allow faster and deeper feeds than either cross-cut or "combination" rip/crosscut blades.

Fig. 17 A low-cost alternative to the static workshop machine is the "site saw". This model is fitted with a sliding carriage and panel support. (Photo: courtesy Sumaco, Elland, Yorks.)

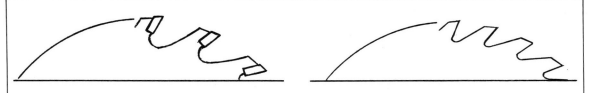

TUNGSTEN CARBIDE TIPPED
(T.C.T.) RIP SAW BLADE

CONVENTIONAL STEEL PLATE
RIP SAW BLADE

Fig. 18 All rip saw blades are designed for fast, deep cutting. The harsh tearing action of a steel rip blade makes it generally unsuitable for any sawing operation other than timber ripping, whereas the cutting action of the T.C.T. equivalent makes it suitable for general conversion duties in a wide variety of materials.

Edge Clearance

For any machine cutting tool to work efficiently, only the actual *cutting edge* of the tool should be making work contact. Work clearance must therefore be provided for the supporting body of the tool in its design. In the case of a circular saw this means that the cut or "kerf" produced by the teeth must be wider than the supporting saw plate (Fig. 19). With steel saws, where the teeth are formed from the plate itself, clearance is achieved by bending, or "setting" alternate teeth laterally. Tipped saws have teeth which are silver-soldered in place and the cutting tips are wider than the saw plate. Clearance, or "relief" bevels are then ground on the sides and top of each tooth (Fig. 20).

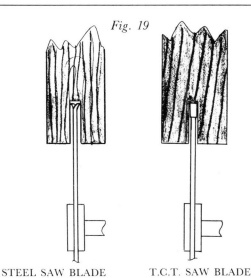

Fig. 19

STEEL SAW BLADE

Plate clearance is provided by alternate lateral setting of successive teeth

T.C.T. SAW BLADE

Plate clearance is achieved by virtue of a wider tip ground back or "relieved" on supporting faces

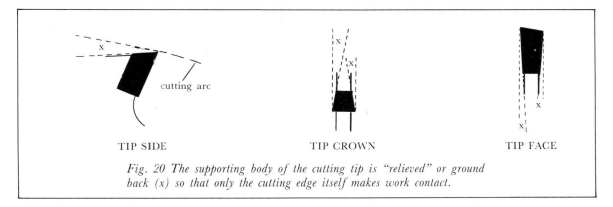

TIP SIDE

TIP CROWN

TIP FACE

Fig. 20 The supporting body of the cutting tip is "relieved" or ground back (x) so that only the cutting edge itself makes work contact.

Some saw blades do not have this plate clearance across the full width of the blade and one side of the plate – *always* the side nearest the rip fence – is tapered-in towards the teeth. This is done to produce a narrower kerf, hence a material saving, when cutting laths for interwoven fencing, etc. A saw blade of this type (swage saw) must never be used for general sawing as a kick-back will almost inevitably result due to material binding on the plate. It is also essential that swage saws are only used with a short rip fence (see RIP SAWING) so that laths cut in this way are free to bend away from the blade immediately they have been severed by the front teeth.) (Fig. 21.)

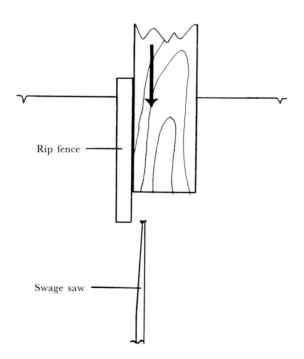

Fig. 21 *Swage saws are used only in the production of thin laths which can bend away from the saw plate as the cut proceeds. It is essential that the rip fence does not extend onto the table beyond the roots of the tooth gullets so as to compress the offcuts between itself and the thickening plate.*

Pitch and Gullet

Pitch is the term used to describe the distance between successive teeth, and to a large extent the gullet, or space between teeth, will be determined by the pitch. (Gullets can be enlarged by grinding *into* the plate.) The gullet area is essential for carrying waste produced by the cutting action of the teeth until it can be discharged by centrifugal force below the level of the workpiece and table as the saw rotates. Large gullets will obviously carry a greater amount of waste than short or shallow gullets where waste will accumulate and tend to interfere with, or block the cutting capabilities of the following tooth – particularly on deep cuts.

Tooth Hook

Hook describes the inclination of a tooth in relation to a radius line from the centre of the saw plate. Rip saws have teeth with a pronounced positive hook (i.e. the teeth are inclined *forward* from their roots), whereas cross-cut and fine pitch blades for board conversion, etc., have teeth angled nearer the radius line and in some cases even inclined backwards, giving them *negative* hook.

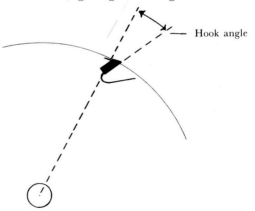

Fig. 22 *"Hook" is the inclination of a tooth face in relation to a radius line. Pronounced positive hook (forward inclination of the tooth as illustrated) makes for faster and easier, but generally rougher cutting.*

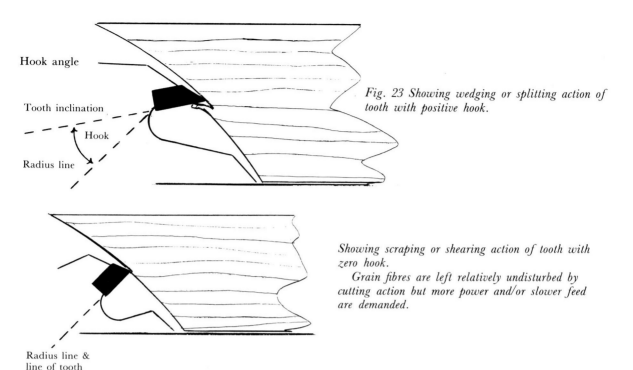

Hook angle

Tooth inclination

Hook

Radius line

Fig. 23 Showing wedging or splitting action of tooth with positive hook.

Showing scraping or shearing action of tooth with zero hook.

Grain fibres are left relatively undisturbed by cutting action but more power and/or slower feed are demanded.

Radius line & line of tooth

Tooth hook dictates the "sharpness" angle of the cutting edge and its angle of entry into the workpiece. Positive hook allows the cutting edge to enter the work with a wedging action and is less demanding of available power, but will give a rougher finish due to the fact that grain fibres will tend to be forced apart by the tip's wedge-like entry. Less positively hooked teeth work with more of a "scraping" attack, give a finer finish, but are very limited in usefulness for general sawing due to the much higher power demand. (Fig. 23.)

Plate Tension

In general, only the teeth of a saw blade should be making contact with the work and a proportion of the energy expended in cutting will unavoidably be converted to heat. The periphery of a blade will therefore tend to warm up more quickly than the main plate body and, if not taken into account,

would cause plate distortion.

To prevent this occurrence, saw plates are "tensioned" during manufacture. This used to be carried out as a highly skilled manual hammering process. (Tensioning by this method is still practised by saw doctors during saw servicing where a plate is found to be "slack" in localized areas.) Modern manufacturers favour the use of highly loaded pressure rollers on either side of the plate while it is slowly rotated to induce diminishing bands of tension from internal to external diameters. This, within limits, allows the plate to expand uniformly in uneven temperature gradients.

A plate which has lost tension will be seen to be throwing from side to side – most noticeably as it slows down after switching off. Such a plate should be returned for servicing.

Tungsten tipped blades in particular have an extremely long service life and to assist the tension factor, slots are often incorporated around the edge of the plate. These allow a degree of independent expansion between segments on the plate edge and also break-up harmonic frequencies, which in some blades can build into an unbearable resonant scream.

Using The Saw Bench

Understandably, inexperienced machine users concentrate attention on the feed side of the saw as this is the area where material is being cut. Injuries occurring at this point due to direct contact with the cutting edge are largely a matter of carelessness and to that extent predictable. In fact, it is the cutter force active at the *back* of the blade which causes most accidents and the operator's concentration must, therefore, be maintained during the entire feed *and* take-off procedure; also at *all* times when the saw is running whether work is being fed or not.

Work, hands or clothing forced against the ascending rear edge of the blade will not simply be cut, but *pulled* onto the blade. (The latest regulations require that factory sited saws with a blade diameter of 450 mm (18″) or more must have at least 1200 mm (48″) of fixed take-off table or support frame behind the blade, primarily for the protection of secondary personnel – such as a "taker-off" – by making accidental contact with the rear of the blade less likely.)

Further consideration of the cutting and rejection forces involved when sawing is also helpful in the development of more-or-less automatic safety-consciousness. The cutting force exerted by the teeth at the point where the workpiece is conventionally fed onto the blade is directed downwards and onto the table. As feed progresses to a point where the work reaches the back of the blade, cutter force which is allowed to influence the workpiece will be lifting it *off* the table and back along the top of the saw directly towards the operator. (Fig. 24).

Provided these forces are understood and *controlled* by proper use of the saw guarding systems, accidents of this type cannot occur.

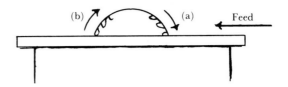

Fig. 24 Cutter force (a) at the feed edge of the blade is tending to force the workpiece downwards onto the table.

Force (b) exerted on work in contact with the rear of the blade is tending to lift the workpiece and reject it in the direction of the operator.

The Riving Knife

This is a steel knife projecting through the table immediately behind the sawblade, contoured to follow the arc of the blade and directly in line with it. The knife should be set as close as possible to the blade (allowing for clearance), and certainly no more than 12 mm ($\frac{1}{2}$″) from it at table level. The riving knife should also have a concave profile so that its curvature more or less matches the curve of the sawblade. Riving knives which also act as the support for the crown guard will automatically extend up to a line above the uppermost teeth of the blade. Otherwise, where the riving knife is independent of the guard, it must project up to a line not less than 25 mm (1″) from the top of the blade or, in the case of large diameter blades (over 600 mm (24″) diameter) to a height of 225 mm (9″) above the table.

The riving knife will give some protection in that its presence prevents direct in-line contact with the rearmost teeth of the saw, but its *primary* purpose is to hold a cut in progress open, and stop partially severed work closing and binding on the ascending rear edge of the blade. The knife should be 10 per cent thicker than the saw plate and this will make it approximately equal in thickness to the width of the saw kerf.

26

(Hardwoods in particular can sometimes "move" quite dramatically as the fibres are severed during ripping, and the kerf may close with considerable pressure on the back of the plate if not checked by the riving knife.) (Fig. 25.)

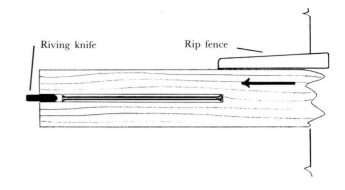

Fig. 25 (right) The riving knife is an **essential** *safety device which holds the kerf (saw cut) open and prevents cut faces closing on the ascending rear edge of the blade.*

The Top Guard

This guard covers the top edge of the sawblade and acts not only to deflect waste and prevent accidental contact with the uppermost teeth, but *also* to check or limit the effects of material rejection. Obviously, there is a point during any feed when the work has progressed to the back of the blade and has not reached the cut-holding protection of the riving knife, and when binding of the material may cause work to be picked-up and rejected. Provided that the top guard has been set properly, the work cannot be kicked-back along the top of the blade towards the operator. The guard must

therefore be set down to cover the gullets of the uppermost teeth and be no more than 12 mm ($\frac{1}{2}''$) above the upper face of the work at the forward cutting edge of the blade.

(Although current U.K. regulations do not require it, my own feelings are that the under-surface of the top guard should be no more than 12 mm ($\frac{1}{2}''$) from the upper face of the work at *any* point along its length. Work that is picked-up at the back of the saw cannot then gather much velocity before being checked by the guard, and at worst a slight chattering of the workpiece will be experienced at this point.)

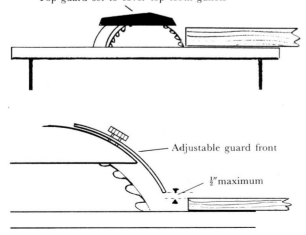

Top guard set to cover top tooth gullets

Adjustable guard front

$\frac{1}{2}''$ maximum

Fig. 26 The top (or crown) guard is often fitted to the riving knife and its height over the sawtable is controlled by the rise and fall mechanism of the saw.
The projection of the blade must then, be set with safety rather than optimum cutting efficiency in mind and clearance between the lower front of the guard and the work surface must be no more than 12mm ($\frac{1}{2}''$).

(Some guards have an adjustable front extension which can be slid down and locked to enable the sawblade to be used at maximum projection. Side flanges extend back to cover the roots and gullets of the teeth.)

Rip-sawing

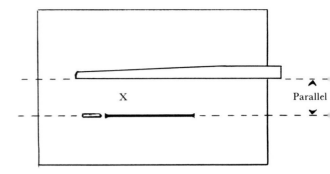

Fig. 27 *Where a long rip fence is used, it* **must** *be parallel with the blade so that work is fed in perfect alignment and no compression occurs at the region marked x. (Feed right to left).*

Converting timber along its length (parallel with the general run of the grain), is effected with the control provided by the rip-fence. Most manufacturers of lightweight sawbenches provide a rip-fence which is *not* suitable for timber ripping as it extends onto the bench to a point well beyond the ideal line, that is, to a point *just* beyond the gullets of the front teeth. Some benches are in fact equipped with rip-fences which extend right along the bench to the take-off edge. Long fences of this type are suitable for the conversion of man-made boards and materials which are intrinsically stable where material movement and kerf binding are unlikely to occur. In deep ripping timber operations however, severed material should be free to move away from the blade once cut so that compression between blade and fence cannot occur. When an extended fence is used, it must be aligned so that it is *absolutely* parallel with the line of the blade, so that work is not forced against either side of the blade's rear edge during feed in an effort to maintain full length fence contact. (Fig. 27.)

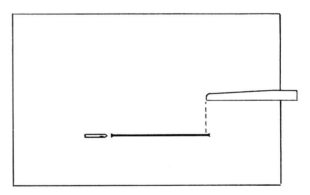

Fig. 28 *The ideal fence for timber ripping is one which extends onto the table to a line just beyond the gullets of the front teeth. This allows severed work to move freely as the feed progresses.*

If a rip-fence of the proper length is not provided for timber work, a simple timber sub-fence can easily be made for attachment to the in-feed end of the existing fence. (Fig. 28.)

There may be a feeling that a short fence of the type recommended provides very little control contact during the final stages of a cut, but in fact, the line of the blade itself and riving knife will hold the line of the cut and professional sawyers often only make use of the actual nose of the rip-fence, rather than its length, for rip feed control, by setting the fence with a very slight amount of "lead-in" to the blade.

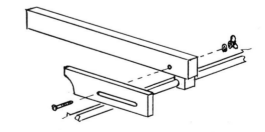

A timber or composite board sub-fence can be made for attachment to a long rip fence. The slot allows for back or forward adjustment to suit various blade height settings.

Push Sticks

Every saw bench must be provided with a push-stick so that the operator's hand does not have to follow a workpiece onto the table beyond the leading edge of the saw blade and thus be in a position between the blade and the fence. A push-stick (or *two* push-sticks, where the outside hand would otherwise have to pass dangerously close to the blade) must *always*, therefore, be to hand for the final part (300 mm/12″) of any ripping operations and for removal of offcuts from the vicinity of the blade.

Fig. 29 (right) Always have at least one push stick to hand for the final part of any feed. A second stick is useful for applying secondary control pressure and/or removing offcuts. (Photo: courtesy J. Fox & Son, Cardiff.)

Cross-cutting

This operation is controlled by means of a sliding mitre fence running in a milled table slot parallel to the blade, or, by supporting the work on a sliding table running level with and alongside the main table. (Fig. 30.)

Apart from general rules and principles previously discussed, the most vital consideration in crosscutting operations is to ensure that offcuts produced are *always* free to move away from the blade once severed. For this reason, THE RIP FENCE SHOULD NEVER BE USED AS A LENGTH-STOP as trapped offcuts may well twist between the blade and fence with *explosive* consequences. Any length stop used should be positioned well clear of the forward cutting edge of the blade. (Fig. 31.)

Fig. 30 A sliding carriage (or dimension table) for crosscutting and panel squaring etc. (Photo: courtesy Startrite Ltd.)

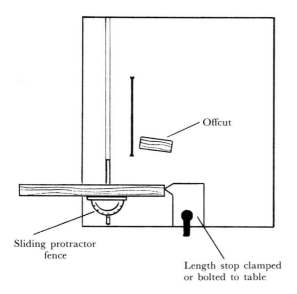

Sliding protractor
fence

Offcut

Length stop clamped
or bolted to table

Fig. 31 *Offcuts produced in crosscutting must* **always** *be free to move away from the blade and the length stop used must be positioned forward of the line of the blade. Offcuts should be removed from the vicinity of the blade using a push stick.*

The Table Insert

All work fed against rotating cutters must be supported by a control surface (or surfaces) as close as possible to the cutter/work contact point. This reduces the leverage forces created by the cutter action and therefore reduces the feed control pressure required for a safe, undeviating line of feed. (Fig. 32.)

To provide this support, saw benches are fitted with a soft metal or hardwood table insert through which the saw blade projects. It should be remembered that not only the *front* part of the aperture provides support for the work as it meets the cutter, but also the *sides* which support work as it moves alongside the cutter. In the case of a saw, thin offcuts may be pulled below the level of

the table and break-up without such support.

A close-fitting insert plate can be made by preparing a piece of hardwood to the pattern of the original insert but without cutting an aperture for the sawblade. With the sawblade wound down below table level, the new insert is secured in the table aperture and the saw run up through it to cut its own aperture which will obviously be of exactly the same width as the blade itself. (The riving knife will almost certainly have to be removed for this operation and the saw bench should not be used until the riving knife has been re-fitted. The new aperture will have to be elongated at the back to make this possible.) If the blade has a 45 degree tilting mechanism, then the freshly cut aperture will have to be enlarged, again by winding up the running blade from below the table, but this time at the new angle.

Obviously care must be taken to ensure that the new insert is *securely* fixed before winding the saw up through it at whatever angle and this operation should not be attempted with sawbenches which have "friction" or spring-clip fixing for their table inserts.

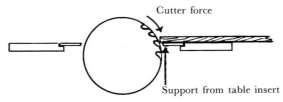

Cutter force

Support from table insert

Fig. 32 (a) *Cutter strike acts to force the work downwards and the workpiece should therefore be supported as closely as possible to the cutting are.*

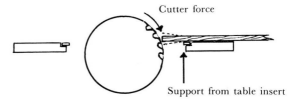

Cutter force

Support from table insert

(b) *Where the workpiece is not supported immediately below and around the point of cutter contact, thin work may whip and splinter.*

Wobble Saws

Saw blades are normally fitted to the drive spindle, or shaft, with flat collars on either side to hold and drive the blade at precisely 90 degrees to the horizontal line of the shaft.

Wobble saws have special collar assemblies with angled contact faces and which allow the saw blade to be pre-set to a slight angle away from the 90 degree vertical whilst still rotating on a horizontal shaft. (Fig. 33). The effect is that the blade throws from side-to-side and cuts a groove wider than the thickness of the blade. Maximum throw or "wobble" in the case of 150 mm (6") diameter wobble-saw will be about 12 mm ($\frac{1}{2}$") so that grooves of any width between the normal saw kerf width 3mm ($\frac{1}{8}$") approx. and this maximum can be pre-set on the outside adjustable collar and cut.

The wobble saw can be useful as an accessory for the sawbench, but most of the operations for which it is required ("blind" cutting and grooving), will have to be run without the standard top guard. Alternative guarding must, therefore, be contrived by the operator for his own safety. This could most simply take the form of a remotely anchored top guard. (Fig. 34.)

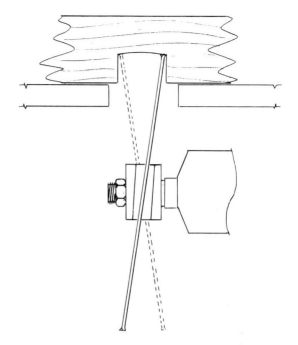

Fig. 33 A wobble saw is mounted between angle faced collar assemblies which can be adjusted to allow the saw to throw laterally. As will be seen from the sketch, the bottom of a groove cut in this way is slightly concave. The dotted line shows the position of the blade when it has rotated through 180°. The intervening space will have been swept by different points on the blade rim.

(a)

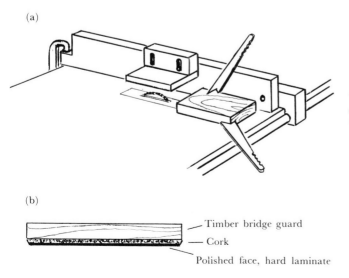

(b)

— Timber bridge guard
— Cork
Polished face, hard laminate

Fig. 34 In circumstances where the normal crown guard has to be removed a bridge guard can be constructed as shown. The new fence is bolted to the rip fence at the feed end and clamped to the work table at the rear or take-off end (a).

Provided the workpiece is of a uniform section the vertically adjustable bridge can be adjusted to act as a work hold-down. 'Slip' can be improved by grooving and silicone waxing the underside of the bridge or by contact gluing a sheet of cork and laminate in place (b). The leading edge of the guard should be radiused to give a lead-in to the work.

31

Moulding Accessories

On some saw benches it is possible to fit a moulding block on the saw spindle in place of the saw blade. Interchangeable pairs of profile cutters can then be clamped in the block as required. Invariably, a different table insert plate will have to be fitted to give support to the workpiece as close as possible to the cutters. Spring guards providing table and fence control pressure should always be used and neither hand should be allowed to pass directly over the cutter block whilst feeding work. Rather, hands should be transferred successively from the infeed to outfeed side of the cutterhead and a push-stick, block or spike should be used for the last part of the feed.

Limitations on the use of a single speed, circular saw bench for moulding operations are experienced in that the cutter-block will be running at only approximately half the optimum rotational speed required for blocks of this type. This will result in a poorer finish and necessitate slow feed speeds to avoid cutter pitch marks. (Feed speeds with a moulding set-up of this type will have to be reduced to around three or four metres (ten or twelve feet) per minute. Even then, the lower peripheral and hence cutter/work impact speed will reduce the dynamic efficiency of the cutting action. To avoid excessive tearing of the grain, therefore, a succession of light cuts should be taken to achieve the full depth of the finished moulding rather than attempting to remove the bulk of the material in one pass.)

It is good practice with *all* unfamiliar machines and cutters to explore their capabilities progressively by using them for light cutting operations. In this way the operator will develop a "feel" for safe working limits. This advice is particularly relevant to the use of moulding machines and tools as the volume of waste machined from the stock in a single pass can be very large indeed and potential material rejection forces are obviously proportional to this.

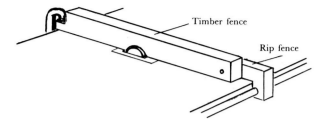

Fig. 34(c) When a moulding block is used in a sawbench the workpiece must be supported against a fence on both the feed and take-off sides of the cutter-block. A timber fence is bolted to the rip fence and clamped to the saw table at the take-off end. The moulding head can then be slowly wound up into the timber fence whilst running (taking care not to foul the metal rip fence), to cut its own working aperture. Only the working part of the cutter is then exposed.

As with all machining operations, no hand should be allowed to pass directly over an unguarded cutter, and bridge or pressure guards must be used.

NOTE: WORK SHOULD NOT BE FED BETWEEN THE CUTTER-BLOCK AND A REMOTE FENCE: – Apart from guarding difficulties, the slightest deviation in feed line will result in a deepening cut and possible loss of feed control. (SEE ALSO "BACK FENCING" WITH THE SPINDLE MOULDER)

*Whenever guarding other than "standard" is made or used, it must obviously be effective. In this context the guard must therefore be **long** enough and **wide** enough to prevent a hand dropping onto the blade accidentally. Shaw type pressure guards could also be used or, for board edge grooving, two boards secured vertically either side of the blade and work fed between them.*

CHAPTER THREE

The Surface Planer and Thicknesser

In most large workshops the surface planer (or "jointer") and the thicknesser are installed as separate, independent machines. With space and cost economy in mind, the two units have been successfully combined as the "planer/thicknesser" – ideally suited to small workshop requirements. Planing and thicknessing are essential machine functions in the preparation of timber sections for almost every woodworking project and it is therefore important that the uses and operational principles of the machines are understood.

Surface planing (also referred to as "overhand planing" or "flatting") is generally a hand-fed operation where work is passed *over* the rotating cutter-block with support and control provided by the two surface tables and fence. Thicknessing is a power-fed operation where work is passed *under* the cutter-block supported on a horizontal, vertically adjustable table, the setting of which controls the uniform thickness of emerging stock. (Some surface planers can be fitted with a thicknessing plate attachment but a much greater demand is placed on the operator in terms of feed support, concentration and physical effort than with the power-fed version of this machine.)

Planer Knives

A choice of knife material may not be available for lightweight planer/thicknessers, but the following information may be useful when cutting performance fails to reach the standards you require.

Most planers are fitted with two or three knives of chrome vanadium steel alloy as standard. (To achieve the optimum of 12,000 cuts per minute, a two-knife block must be driven at 6,000 rpm whereas a three-knife block could be driven at a reduced speed of 4,000 rpm. Of course work/cutter impact speed is also important and there is a definite limit to how much cutter-block speed may be reduced by adding knives without adversely affecting performance. Multi-knife blocks also demand a great deal of care in setting-up as excess projection on just one knife will result in that being the only knife which makes work contact and cuts per minute being reduced from 12,000 to 4,000 in the case of a three-knife block and just 3,000 cuts per minute in the case of a four-knife block.)

Chrome vanadium steel is suitable for machining all softwoods and the "non-abrasive" hardwoods. (Some timbers, although not necessarily hard in texture, are nevertheless, known by machinists as "edge takers". Teak is one such example and chrome steel knives will lose their edge in a matter of ten minutes or so when used for planing this and similarly abrasive timbers. English oak, on the other hand, is texturally

Fig. 35 A combined "over and under" planer/
thicknesser suitable for heavy use. (Photo: courtesy
Multico Ltd., Redhill, Surrey.)

Fig. 36   PLANER/THICKNESSER

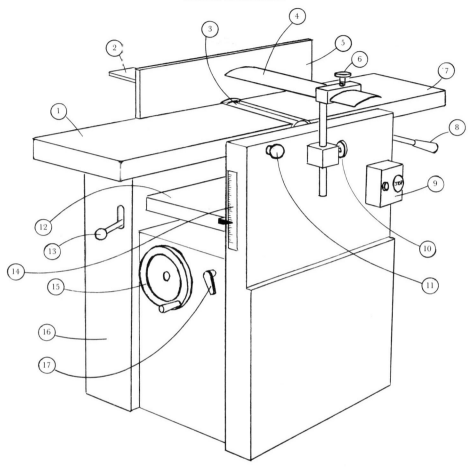

1 Rear table (also called: out-feed table and take-off table)
2 Rear fence guard (also called rear cutterblock guard)
3 Cutterblock (also called planer block)
4 Adjustable bridge guard (also: surfacing guard)
5 Surfacing fence
6 Horizontal (guard) clamp
7 Feed table (also: in-feed table, front table)
8 Feed table height adjuster.
9 ON/OFF switch (also: push button starter)

10 Vertical (guard) clamp
11 Rear table hinge lock (rear table hinged or removeable)
12 Thicknessing bed or table
13 Thicknessing feed isolator (either electrical or mechanical)
14 Thicknesser scale
15 Thicknessing bed vertical adjustment
16 Cabinet (must enclose all chain drives, belts and non-working arc of cutterblock etc.)
17 Height adjustment lock (for thicknessing bed)

harder than teak but less abrasive and consequently kinder to cutters.)

Moving up in steel hardness (and cost), we come to High Speed Steel – abbreviated as HSS. This is a cobalt steel alloy, sometimes with a percentage of tungsten added. It is extremely hard and in industry is used extensively in the manufacture of tools for cutting and turning other softer steels. Obviously, therefore, it will be more suitable for machining timbers of all types than the chrome steel compounds. It should be noted, however, that some species of hardwood either draw-up or produce on their own account gritty substances of such extreme hardness that sparks can be seen at the cutter impact point. Where timbers of

this type are likely to be used for a substantial part of production time, solid or tipped tungsten carbide cutters will be found the most economical.

Tungsten carbide is the only tool compound which is suitable for machining man-made boards which are generally of resin-bonded particle or laminated construction and will take the edge off steel tools in a matter of seconds.

Where feasible, machinists prefer to use HSS cutters rather than tungsten for two reasons: firstly, the cutting edge of a steel cutter can be "freshened-up" by honing with an oilstone, whereas tungsten tools will almost always have to be mechanically re-ground with diamond or Borazon coated wheels. Secondly, and importantly from the machinists' standpoint, a keener cutting edge (therefore better finish) can be induced with steel compounds than with tungsten carbide. The reason for this is that steel compounds are smelted and shaped by rolling or forging whilst the metal is close to its melting point. The molecules of the compound flow and align themselves in response to this pressure giving the material maximum strength and edge-holding capability in certain planes – rather like the run and strength of timber grains. Tungsten carbide, on the other hand, is a "sintered" compound. The fine-grain powder from which the cutter will eventually be made is compressed in a mould (corresponding to the "blank", un-edged cutter shape required) under extremely high temperature and pressure to form a solid block. Unlike steel however, the compound does not flow and always retains a granular structure which, although being of extreme hardness and having qualities of abrasion resistance, is brittle and will tend to chip rather than deform if abused.

Fig. 37 An independent thicknesser. (Photo: courtesy Multico Ltd., Redhill, Surrey.)

It is also relevant that the brittle nature of tungsten carbide necessitates a more obtuse "sharpness" angle to give support to the cutting edge and this will make it generally less satisfactory for working softwoods than an equivalent steel knife which can be ground to a more acute sharpness angle. (See Fig. 38 below.)

Fig. 38(a) Steel and steel alloy knives can be ground to a comparatively acute sharpness angle and can be honed to a superfine edge by the operator. Such knives are particularly suitable for planing softwoods.

(b) Tungsten Carbide or Tungsten Carbide Tipped knives are much harder and have excellent resistance to the abrasive properties of some hardwoods. They are, however, ground to a more obtuse (blunter) sharpness angle so that the bevel can give more support to and minimize chipping of the brittle cutting edge.

(c) Although the inclination (see 'hook' angle re. circular saws) of the knives cannot be altered in the cutter block, the same result (i.e. reducing the wedging and splitting action of knives on wild grain timber) can be achieved by grinding a secondary chamfer on the face of the knife. The angle has been exaggerated for clarity and a relatively small amount of metal at around 15° to the face need only be ground away to achieve the shearing action necessary for difficult timbers. (Only the lightest cuts can be taken with such modified edges because of the increased power demand.)

Knife setting

Understanding how the surface planer works is helpful when setting-up the machine as correct procedures become obvious. When feeding work over the cutterblock, the amount of stock removed is determined by the setting of the infeed table. Lowering the infeed table increases the depth of cut. Raising the infeed table reduces the depth of cut. The planer knives should be no higher than the level of the take-off (or outfeed) table at the highest point in their rotational arc and therefore, if the infeed table is raised to the same level as the outfeed, no cut will be taken. If the infeed table is lowered by 3 mm ($\frac{1}{8}$"), then the knives will plane off 3 mm ($\frac{1}{8}$") and the reduced stock will flow freely onto the support of the outfeed table. The series of illustrations in Figure 39 make this clearer.

If the knives have been set too high in the cutter-block, (i.e. above the level of the take-off table at their highest rotational position) then too much stock will have been planed away and there will be a gap between the workpiece and surface of the take-off table. At some point during the feed, when control pressure is transferred from infeed to outfeed tables, the line and accuracy of the cut will be lost as the work drops to take up the gap. If the knives have been set too low in the

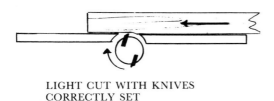

LIGHT CUT WITH KNIVES CORRECTLY SET

Fig. 39(a) If the knives have been correctly set so that they are level with the plane of the take-off table they will always remove sufficient material from the work being fed that it flows freely and directly onto the support of that table.

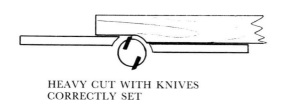

HEAVY CUT WITH KNIVES CORRECTLY SET

(b) The amount of stock removed in a single pass is controlled solely by the setting of the in-feed table and the constant height relationship between knife height and out-feed table is unaffected. In this illustration the in-feed table has been lowered to increase stock removal and as in (a) above the work flows directly onto the support of the take-off table.

KNIVES SET TOO HIGH

(c) If the knives have been set too high in the block, an excess of stock will be removed and the work will not receive immediate support from the take-off table. The line and accuracy of the operation will be lost. (This fault in setting is most readily detected by the appearance of a depressed step at the tail end of the surface planed which will be exactly the width of the aperture.)

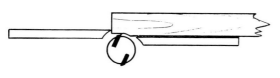

KNIVES SET TOO LOW

(d) Where knives have been set too low in the block and are below the level of the take-off table at the highest point in their rotational arc, the feed will be checked by the lip of that table. Lifting the nose of the work over the obstruction to continue the feed will again result in the loss of the true planing line.

cutter-block, they will not machine away sufficient material for the work to pass over the lip of the outfeed table and the cut will be checked until the operator pushes or lifts the workpiece over the obstruction and again the line of the cut will be lost.

To check that knives are set to the correct height, a timber straight-edge should be used. This is held on the take-off table with one end projecting over the cutter-block aperture. The block is then rotated by hand so that each knife in turn passes through the top part of its cutting arc. If the knives have been correctly set, they should *just* make contact with the overhang of the straight-edge and pull it forward about 3 mm ($\frac{1}{8}''$) before losing contact again. (Fig. 40.) Knives should be checked for the correct projection setting at both ends and re-checked after the final tightening of the clamping wedges. On lightweight machines in particular, it is unusual to get the setting right first time and several successive adjustments will often be necessary to compensate for projection variation caused by "pinch-tight" and "fully-tight" clamp pressure.

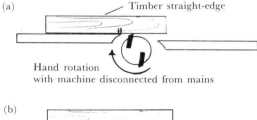
(a) Timber straight-edge

Hand rotation with machine disconnected from mains

(b)

Fig. 40 CHECKING PLANER KNIFE SETTINGS: A timber straight-edge is held loosely on the take-off table as illustrated. Two pencil marks about 3mm ($\frac{1}{8}''$) apart are made on the side of the straight-edge with the foremost mark lined up on the lip of the table(a).

Rotating the cutterblock by hand, the knife being checked should barely make contact with the underside of the straight-edge and pull it forward no more than 3mm ($\frac{1}{8}''$) before losing contact as the hand rotation continues (b).

Each knife should be checked at both ends.

It is always sound practice to DOUBLE CHECK the security of knife locking clamps after final projection checks have been made, as knives hidden below the aperture have occasionally been left loose. Also, mating components in the block assembly should be cleaned of resin deposits etc. so that firm and positive contact is made on clamping. Some manufacturers already employ a positive cutter retention system which relies on mechanical interlocking of the cutter/block or wedge faces in addition to normal clamping pressure. This is not yet a legal requirement in the U.K. but it seems likely that it will eventually become so. (Fig. 41.)

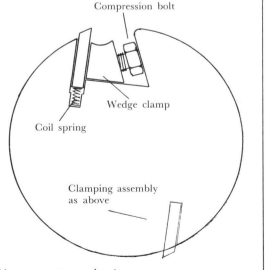

Compression bolt

Wedge clamp

Coil spring

Clamping assembly as above

Fig. 41 Typical planer block knife locking arrangement showing spring loaded knife seatings, wedge clamps and compression bolts.

Using The Surface Planer

Surface planers are sometimes called "jointers" because they are capable of shooting a long, true edge which can be butt-jointed to a corresponding edge (as in panel construction). Long surface tables are a definite advantage for this operation in that they control the constancy of feed attitude. To illustrate this in the extreme, it would be very difficult indeed to maintain *precisely* horizontal manual feed of a 2 metres (6 ft) length of timber on surface tables of, say,

150 mm (6″) in length. The longer the tables, the more supporting control surface available and the less likelihood of feed attitude variance. (Industrial surface planers may have a combined surface table length of 2.4 metres (8 ft) or more to speed production and decrease dependence on operator skill.)

The first operation in surfacing is to plane one of the broad faces of the work. If there is any noticeable concavity, either in the width or in the length of the workpiece, then

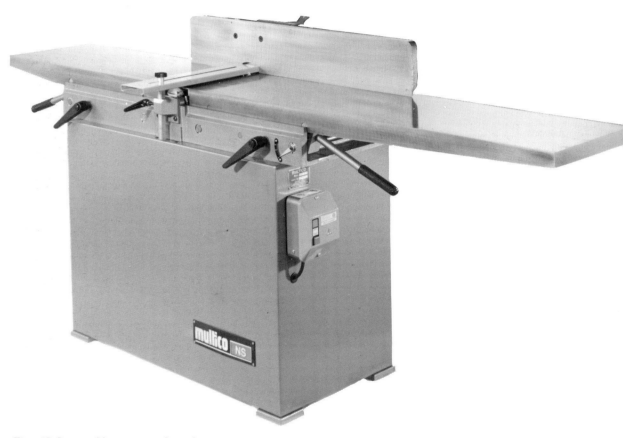

Fig. 42 Long tables on a surface planer are advantageous in enabling the work to be fed in a consistent attitude relative to the cutters. This becomes especially important when attempting to straighten boards "in wind" (i.e. twisted along their length). (Photo: courtesy Multico Ltd., Redhill, Surrey.)

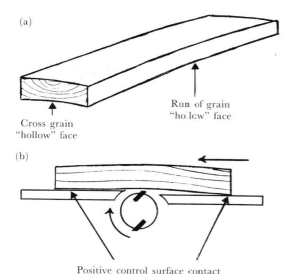

(a)

Cross grain
"hollow" face

Run of grain
"hollow" face

(b)

Positive control surface contact

Fig. 43(a) Where sawn timber has moved significantly in drying, one face and/or edge may be slightly concave or "hollow". This is the side which should be planed first.

(b) When surfacing the "hollow" face or edge of a workpiece the planer may "run out of cut" during the feed but successive feeds will produce a true surface line.

Attempting to surface plane a **convex** face on the other hand is much more difficult as the work can rock on the control surfaces during feed.

it is this face (the "hollow" face) which should be planed in preference to a convexly distorted face. (Fig. 43.)

Some timbers – particularly hardwoods – may have a pronounced grain bias when viewed from the side and best results will be obtained if the timber is presented to the surfacer with the grain running predominantly from upper front to lower rear (Fig. 44). In the case of very wild or

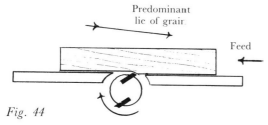

Predominant
lie of grain

Feed

Fig. 44

stripey grains, it may be difficult to decide which is the predominant lie and a light cut in both directions with visual comparison of the surfaces produced will provide the answer.

When planing the broad face of a workpiece the guard should be set so that it extends over the full width of the cutter-block to the fence and the timber has therefore to pass underneath it with minimal clearance. The operator's hands should pass in turn *over* the guard as feed progresses. (Fig. 45.)

Fig. 45(a) & (b) When planing a narrow edge (45b), work passes between the guard and the fence. The guard is set as close as possible to the cutterblock and the work.

Squaring

Having planed one broad face, the next step is to "square" the timber. The term is used in this context to describe the action of planing an adjacent face (or edge) at 90 degrees to the previously planed face. The fence now becomes the primary control surface as it alone can provide vertical support. In other words, feed control pressure must now be directed against the vertical face of the fence to hold the planed broad face flush against it during the entire feed of the narrow face over the cutter-block (Fig. 46). Provided that the fence has been set accurately to 90 degrees, the narrow face will have been planed at exactly that angle in relationship to the broad face. (Few small planers have positive and accurate angle stops with which to set their fences. Unless you know that your machine's accuracy can be relied upon it is best to use a square or template to set the fence to any critical angle.)

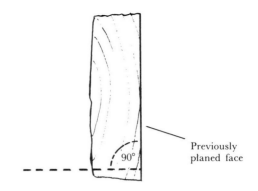

Fig. 46(a) "Squaring" simply means planing two adjacent faces to a 90° relationship. Material below the dotted line must be accurately machined away.

(b) Work is fed between the fence and the bridge guard ensuring that the previously planed face is held firmly against the vertical face of the fence.

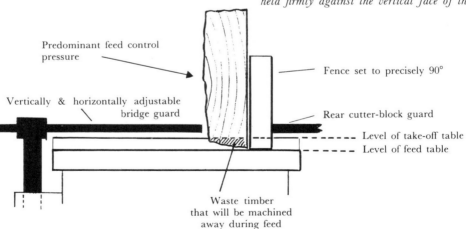

If the work is particularly wide or thin, then it will be best to square both edges in relation to the broad face that has been surfaced before moving onto the next stage of "thicknessing" – this, for reasons that are made clear in the following section.

For squaring operations the guard must be set down as low as possible over the exposed part of the cutterblock and as close as possible to the work face so that clearance between the guard, work and cutter-block is at no point more than 10 mm ($\frac{3}{8}''$).

Bevel or chamfer planing of edges can be carried out on the surface planer by using the fence at the chosen angle. However, firm fence contact becomes increasingly difficult to maintain as the angle of the fence is set further away from the vertical. This is because the direction from which table pressure and fence pressure have to be applied are closer together (Fig. 47). It is also important that the guard be *rigidly* fixed for this operation to prevent any likelihood of the work slipping underneath it into a suddenly heavier cut. Where possible, it is best to remove bulk waste by sawing and use the planer for final finishing. In fact, because of the potential dangers outlined above, the current draft for the U.K. regulations covering this operation recommends that a second fence be employed which runs the full length of the table to prevent work slipping down off the main fence, or, that the operation be carried out with a jig on the thicknessing bed – as described in the following section.

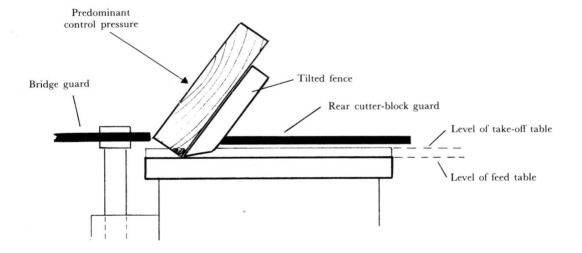

*Fig. 47 Bevel or chamfer planing should preferably be carried out close to the edge of the tables and with a **rigidly** fixed guard set as closely as possible to the work face. If successive passes over the cutter-block are necessary to remove the required depth of material, the guard should be re-set as appropriate to ensure that it remains correctly positioned.*
*(**Note**: Planing chamfers or bevels would normally be carried out after the work has been squared and thicknessed).*

Fig. 48 Horizontal and vertical pressure shoes ("Shaw" guards) must be used to control work being rebated on a surface planer and to prevent the operator's hands passing directly over the cutter-block. (Photo: courtesy Startrite Ltd., Gillingham, Kent.)

Thicknessing

It may seem at first glance that since one corner of a workpiece can be squared on the surface planer, there is no good reason why all four corners should not be squared and a "thicknesser" be, perhaps, unnecessary. Certainly, all four faces can be planed at 90 degrees to each other, but the workpiece might still be tapered in its length and of different dimensions at each end. The thicknesser not only produces work of uniform sectional dimension throughout the length of the timber, but also achieves this in a fraction of the time possible by any other method.

The action of the thicknesser is to plane opposite faces parallel to and uniformly distant from each other along the full length of the workpiece (Fig. 49). As the squared faces have already been planed, it is these which are presented to the thicknessing bed in turn and their opposite faces (i.e. the unplaned faces) which are machined during thicknessing. The importance of accurate preparatory squaring now becomes evident. Should the squared angle be anything other than 90 degrees, the diagonally opposite angle will be reproduced with the same error (Fig. 50).

During thicknessing the work is supported on a vertically adjustable bed and fed automatically by power driven rollers under the cutter-block. The pre-set distance between the bed and the cutters will be the thickness of stock produced as it flows through the machine. (If there is any movement of the bed due to backlash or play in the height-adjusting mechanism, then the bed may alter height in response to varying spring pressure from the feed rollers and a slight step in the ends of the workpiece be noticed. On most thicknessers there will be found a bed clamping control to prevent this.) A calibrated scale at the infeed end of the bed will give a guide to the height setting but it should be checked for accuracy before being relied upon. Simply feed a piece of timber through the unit, measure its actual thickness after machining and set the scale pointer accordingly.

(a)

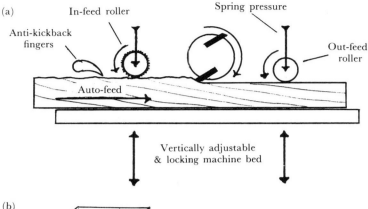

Anti-kickback fingers

In-feed roller

Spring pressure

Out-feed roller

Auto-feed

Vertically adjustable & locking machine bed

Fig. 49(a) The thicknesser produces work of a uniform section dimension throughout the length of the workpiece.

***Note**: The entire assembly of cutterblock, feed rollers and other moving parts above the feed path of the work must be enclosed by a guard that prevents any possibility of accidental contact. In the case of combined planer/thicknessers this may be partly effected by the surfacing tables and/or a separate hood which serves the same purpose.*

(b)

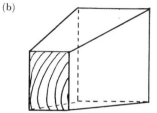

(b) An extreme illustration of work which has been "squared" on all four faces but it is not of uniform section. At any point along the length of the work a section would show that each face is at 90° to its neighbour but obviously opposite faces are not parallel.

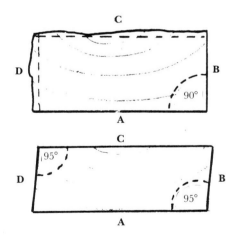

C

D

B

90°

A

Fig. 50(a) Faces A and B have been squared on the surface planer. Face A will be offered to the thicknesser bed and the upper face C will be automatically planed parallel across its width and throughout its length. Face B will then be offered to the bed and D planed parallel.

C

D

95°

B

95°

A

(b) The importance of accurate squaring before thicknessing is obvious in this illustration. The angle that was surface planed between faces A and B in the squaring operation will be reproduced between faces C and D diagonally opposite.

Feeding The Thicknesser

The thicknesser is likely to be the only power-fed machine in a home workshop and should do more to convince its owner of the value of automation than any amount of reading. The comparison between manual and automatic feeds becomes even more dramatic if you have experienced working with both alternatives on similar machines. Early in my woodworking life, the only thicknesser I had was a thicknessing plate attachment for my small surfacer. To plane and thickness frame and panel components for an average fitted kitchen used to take my partner and myself the best part of a working day. Our first power-fed "over and under" was purchased after three years of head-scratching about the cost. In the event, pressure of work forced us to make the decision and we wondered how on earth we had managed without a planer/thicknesser for all those years. Jobs that used to take two of us a day could now be done by one of us in a single morning. In his book *Machine Woodworking*, John Clayton states, that in his personal experience, the addition of power feed to some machines can increase production by as much as *five hundred* percent! He quotes the vertical spindle moulder as one such example, and I would certainly agree. Power feed reduces the need for operator skill, increases the safety of any operation and will produce consistent results. Independent power feed attachments are now available for fitting to spindle moulders, saws and surface planers which have sufficiently strong tables (cast iron). There are some precautions which the operator should take, however, and these are dealt with below.

In the case of a thicknesser, two spring-loaded feed rollers, one on either side of the cutter-block, grip the work and drive it through the machine at a pre-set speed (usually around 6 metre (20 ft) per minute in the case of light and medium weight machines). The in-feed roller is heavily splined to provide maximum grip without excessive spring pressure and consequent binding of the workpiece as it slides along the bed. The out-feed roller is smooth or only slightly knurled so as not to mark the surface of the work just thicknessed. Less grip is required on the out-feed because at the stage during feed when the work has left the grip and drive of the in-feed roller, it will also be nearly half way off the thicknessing bed and frictional resistance will therefore be that much less.

Depending on the spread of in-feed roller pressure (put another way, the width of the face being fed), and the hardness of the timber, small indentations will have pressed into the surface of the workpiece. The cutters must, therefore, remove a certain minimum of material if these indentations are to be machined away. This makes the thicknesser

generally unsuitable for taking the very light finishing cuts necessary to avoid tearing on difficult and wild-grain timbers. The problem is best handled by leaving a somewhat "full" dimension on thicknessing, and finishing with very light cuts on the surfacer.

After work has been entered into the thicknesser, the feed rollers take over and the operator's function is one of supporting any overhang. Since it is the feed rollers which now provide downward pressure to keep the work in contact with the bed, it is important that they are allowed to make firm contact with the work. This may not be possible if two pieces are being fed through the unit simultaneously. If there is any discrepancy between the pre-machined thickness of the two pieces, then the thinner of the two may well not be in contact with the controlling pressure of the infeed roller. This is extremely dangerous and the rule must be FEED ONE PIECE AT A TIME. Even if the pieces appear to be of equal thickness before machining to a new dimension this rule must be complied with as either piece may be made effectively thicker by riding up on a waste chip and feed roller contact be lost on the other piece. (The only exception to this rule is in the case of larger industrial thicknessers which have segmented feed rollers.)

If the work to be thicknessed has any noticeably thick sections along its length or is thicker at one end than the other, this should be taken into account when setting the height of the thicknessing bed. For example, if the bed has been set to a height such that it will be machining a couple of millimetres from the *thinner* end of a tapered length, the unit will be subjected to a progressively deepening cut if it is fed thin end first and will jam if this exceeds the machine's capabilities or shatter the work if the cut becomes too heavy for the remaining body of the work to support. Should you inadvertently get into this situation, the best course is to wind down the thicknessing bed as quickly as possible, or, if the machine has a separate feed isolator control, disengage the feed. Switching off the power to the cutter-block whilst heavy feed is in progress should only be considered as a last resort in the case of emergency (see below), as it is effectively the same as a jam through overload and may have the same consequences of kick-back or work shattering. (Fig. 51.)

Fig. 51 (below) The level of the thicknesser bed must be set with the thickest section of an irregular workpiece in mind. Several passes may often be necessary to reduce irregular work to an even thickness.

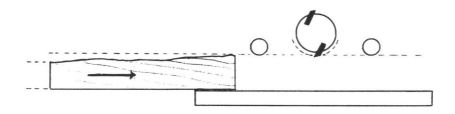

Power-fed machines *should* have a feed isolator within easy reach of the operator, but this is not always the case where machines do not have to comply with Health & Safety regulations. If your machine does not have this protection fitted, it is in your own interests to ensure that at least the ordinary ON/OFF switch, or an extension to it, is fitted on the thicknesser feed end of the machine as well as the surfacer feed end.

Fingers or clothing may be caught up with the work, and, although it shouldn't happen if the TEN GENERAL RULES in Chapter One are observed, there may be insufficient take-off space for the work to leave the machine. (A person employed in taking-off from a power-fed machine could also be in considerable danger of being trapped when working long lengths in confined workshop areas.)

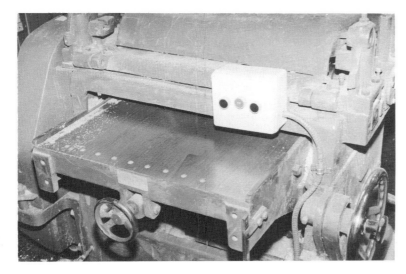

Fig. 52 The STOP switch on all machines must be easily within the operator's reach and particularly so in the case of automatic feeds. Older machines such as this thicknesser may have to be modified to meet this requirement. (Photo: courtesy J. Fox & Sons, Cardiff.)

Anti-kick-back Protection

An essential safety feature of the thicknesser is the anti-kick-back device. This is a bar extending across the in-feed aperture in front of and level with the in-feed roller. Mounted on the bar are pawls which ride up as the work passes underneath them but drop and lock into the face of the workpiece if there is a kick-back and prevent it being ejected from the machine. Of course the kick-back protection will only be effective in preventing rejection of the bulk timber and will afford very little protection from splinters if the work breaks up. It is sensible, therefore, not to look directly into the feed aperture when the machine is in operation. Also, of course, the movement of the pawls may in time become restricted due to a build up of waste and their freedom to operate efficiently should be regularly checked and cleaned as necessary.

Minimum Lengths

Work passing through a thicknesser (or over a surface planer), must be planed predominantly *with* the run of the grain and not across it. Apart from the fact that cross-grain planing will give a very poor finish, the broad contact area of the cutters and consequent cutter force may cause the work to break up or fracture at the tail end of the cut through lack of cohesive strength in the grain fibres when machined in this direction (Fig. 53).

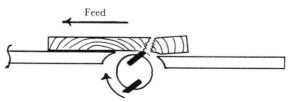

Fig. 53 **Do Not Plane Timber Across the Grain**. *The cutter force in cross-grain planing operations may well exceed the strength of the bond between the grain fibres resulting in the work breaking up.*

Although this may seem fairly straightforward and obvious, occasions may arise during thicknessing when the work tries to turn under the action of the feed rollers and, if too short to be checked, may well end up cross-grained under the cutter-block where it will almost certainly shatter. The point made here is that if the workpiece is *longer* than the width of the feed aperture, it *cannot* turn under the block, even if it has entered the thicknesser beyond a point where manual correction of feed attitude is still possible.

If work of less than the feed aperture width of the thicknesser *must* be thicknessed, it is essential that guide laths are fitted to provide a feed channel on the bed which will not permit the work to turn (Fig. 54).

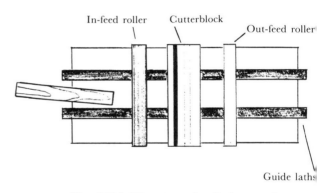

Fig. 54(a) *Plan view of a thicknesser showing guide laths clamped to the bed. These serve two important purposes when thicknessing workpieces which are shorter than the width of the thicknessing bed. Firstly, the work cannot now turn cross-grained under the cutterblock. Secondly the work cannot lose contact with the feed rollers whilst under the block (see also fig. 55).*

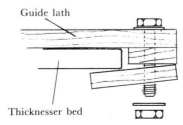

(b) *A simple method of attaching ancillary fences etc. to a machine bed or table. (The bolt head can of course be recessed if required.)*

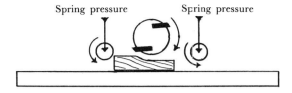

Fig. 55 Work must always be of sufficient length to be in firm contact with one of the feed rollers at all times that it is under the cutter-block. In the example shown the work has left the control of the in-feed roller before reaching the out-feed roller. The cutters may pick the work up as a consequence with damaging and possibly dangerous results.

In addition to the foregoing restriction on the thicknessing of short lengths, it must be clearly understood by the operator that under *no* circumstances should the work be shorter than the outside extremities of the in-feed and out-feed rollers. (If work is trapped between the feed rollers it will be in loose contact with the cutters – but not for long!) (Fig. 55). Unless a large number of short lengths are required, when the time involved in jigging the operation becomes an acceptably small proportion of the total, it is far better to machine in long lengths and crosscut to the required size.

Chamfering & Bevelling With The Thicknesser

Bevels and chamfers of any angle and any width up to that of the thicknesser can be produced with this machine using a "carrier" bed. This is a laterally inclined bed, fitted to the main bed and which allows work to be carried under the cutter-block at the chosen angle (Fig. 56). The carrier bed can be extended at one or both ends and fitted with a locating lip which makes attachment to the main bed a simple matter of clamping or bolting.

The main problem with this type of bed is that it will generally have been made by the operator from the most convenient material – probably timber – and frictional resistance to the feed force may be excessive. The best solution to this problem is to line the bed with a plastic laminated material such as 'Formica' and wax it with a silicone polish. (*All* machine beds, of whatever material, will benefit from cleaning and lubrication with a non-staining silicone based polish.)

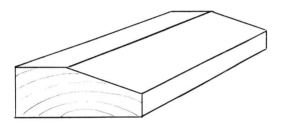

Fig. 56(a) Wide chamfers or bevels can be produced accurately and safely in a succession of passes on an inclined carrier bed fixed to the thicknesser bed.

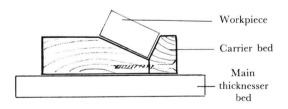

Workpiece

Carrier bed

Main thicknesser bed

(b) The carrier bed should be made slightly longer than the thicknesser bed to provide a projection at either end for clamping (see 54b). "Slip" can be improved by lining the feed channel with a hard laminate.

End-grain Planing

In some instances it can be useful to make use of the planer for finishing end-grain although personally, I would prefer to saw and sand. If the planer is used in this way, it should be the surface planer and *not* the thicknesser where the cut cannot be reversed (see Fig. 57) and fracturing and rejection of the rearmost portion of the work is likely to occur. Planing of end-grain sections having a length of less than four times the width of the table aperture should not be attempted as there will be insufficient contact of work to tables to ensure a stable feed. The use of a right angle push block will also help to keep the work in the vertical position as it passes over the cutters and prevent the work from dipping into a heavier cut.

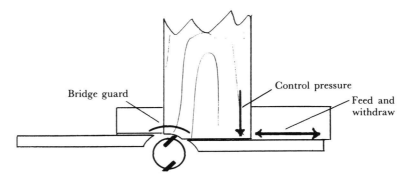

Fig. 57(a) The first step in planing end grain is to plane a small amount of material from one end of the edge only. The work is then withdrawn.

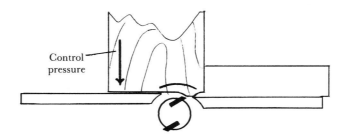

(b) The work is then reversed and the feed recommenced and continued from the opposite end. The cutters do not now break out through a cross-grained edge.

Note: *(1) The edge being planed must be at least four times the width of the cutter aperture so that adequate control surface contact can be maintained.*
(2) Only the lightest cuts should be taken.
(3) The work must be fed over the cutterblock between the guard and the fence as for normal edge planing.
(4) A vertically faced push-block can be used to good effect in feeding the work accurately and ensuring that neither the nose nor tail end of the work dips into the cutter aperture.

CHAPTER FOUR

The Spindle Moulder

Once its capabilities and working principles are understood, the vertical spindle moulder will prove to be one of the most useful machines in any workshop. Many small wood-machining businesses have, in fact, just one each of the classic cutting and planing machines, but *several* spindle moulders permanently set up for rebating, sash jointing, laminate edge trimming, panel fielding and so on.

Years ago, before the Factory Inspectorate had been given the relevant legislative authority and back-up, spindle moulders gained something of a fearsome reputation in the trade and, it must be said, not without reason at that time. Since then, great advances have been made, both in tooling standards and in the adoption of safe working practices. As a result, the vertical spindle moulder is as safe as any other machine – given the understanding and common-sense approach of its operator. For the newcomer to woodmachining, an important factor, as with all machinery, is to explore the machine's potential *progressively*, starting with light cutting operations on sub-stantial workpieces to develop a 'feel' for the cutting forces involved and confidence in the predictability of every pass over the cutters.

The machine itself consists of a horizontal work table through the centre of which projects a verticle spindle that can be wound up or down below table level. Various cutting tools can be fitted to this spindle. Work is guided

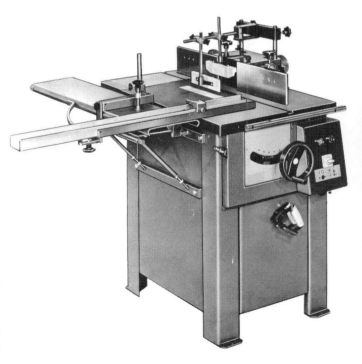

Fig. 58 A good quality, economically priced spindle moulder with sliding carriage. This model offers three speeds so that a wide range of tooling can be safely used. (Also incorporated in this particular unit is a circular saw, further increasing its usefulness in small workshops.) (Photo: courtesy Luna Tools & Machinery Ltd., Milton Keynes.)

Fig. 59

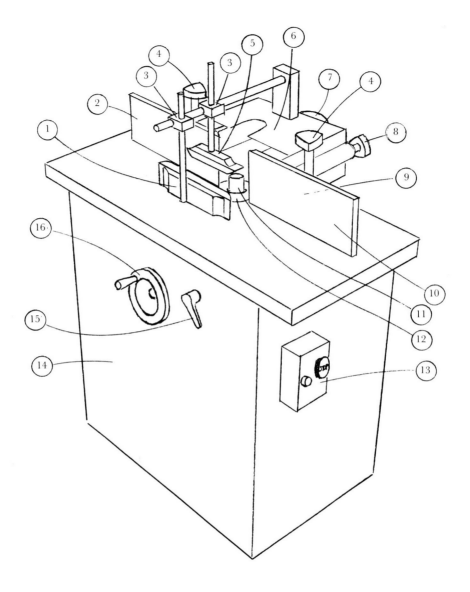

(Nos. 1–10 Removeable fence/guard assembly)

1 Horizontal pressure shoe
2 Outfeed fence (also: take-off fence)
3 Universal clamp

4 Guard assembly table clamp

5 Vertical pressure shoe (also: hold-down shoe)
6 Cutter enclosure/fixed guard
7 Waste outlet (also: extraction duct)
8 Micro-adjuster (also fitted to out-feed fence-not shown)

9 Fence clamp (also fitted to out-feed fence – not shown)
10 Infeed fence

11 Vertical spindle (also: spindle or shaft)
12 Table insert (also: aperture insert or insert ring)
13 ON/OFF switch (also: push button starter)
14 Cabinet (must enclose all drives and moving parts)
15 Spindle height setting clamp
16 Spindle rise and fall adjuster

across the selected cutter with support from the table and two fences, one either side of the cutter. The projection of the cutter through the aperture between the two feed fences is governed by moving the entire fence assembly backwards or forwards and clamping it to the table in the required position. (Fig. 60.)

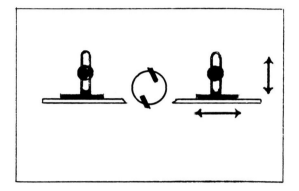

Fig. 60 Both fences also have lateral adjustment so that they can be brought as close as possible to the cutter arc.

Tooling

"Tooling" is the collective term applied to cutters and cutter holding devices. In the case of the spindle moulder it is worth knowing that by far the biggest range of standard and specialized tooling is available with a 30 mm bore size. Other bore sizes are available, but very often these are a sleeved or bored-out adaptation of the 30 mm standard and are consequently more expensive and less readily available. The two principal types of cutting tool used in conjunction with spindle moulders are the "block with interchangeable cutters" pattern and the "solid profile block" described in the following sections.

Block & Cutters

The moulding block is a circular tool with slots machined into its body on opposite sides, into which balanced pairs of moulding cutters can be fitted. In circumstances where the demand on the spindle moulder is highly varied and production at any one time is likely to be no more than a few thousand metres of a particular moulding, this pattern of tool is most economical.

The cutters are held in the block by a clamping device similar to that used for clamping planer knives (Fig. 61). Projection of the cutters may be adjustable or pre-set against the machined seating in the block. The setting of adjustable cutters can be carried out with the block in position on the spindle and simply bringing up one of the feed fences so that one of the cutters barely makes contact with it when the block is

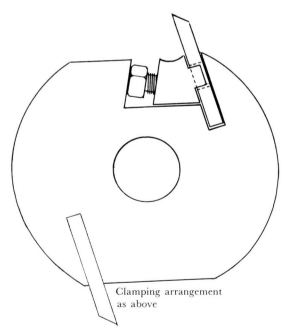

Clamping arrangement as above

Fig. 61 Typical moulding block with interchangeable cutters. Blocks of this type are becoming increasingly popular as they incorporate the additional clamping security of a peg protruding from the mating face of the wedge which enters a hole in the cutter.

rotated by hand. Turn the block through 180 degrees and adjust the projection of the other cutter to the same extent. Finally, check the security of both cutters and withdraw the fences to give minimal working clearance (Fig. 62).

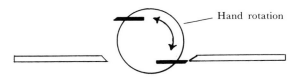

Fig. 62 Checking cutter projection against one of the feed fences. Even if the cutters are not of the fully adjustable type, some tolerance in the seating will allow fractional adjustment.

Always make such adjustments with the machine disconnected from the mains and check clamp security before reconnection.

Cutters of the interchangeable type are sharpened by grinding and honing on the bevel face and it is important to maintain profile balance for working efficiency. If imbalance in not just the shape, but also the *weight* of the cutter, becomes excessive then the resulting vibration will place a considerable and unnecessary strain on the shaft bearings and affect the safety of feed operations due to vibration being transmitted through the table and control fences to the workpiece. (Some suppliers sell profile cutters singly and advise the use of a "balancing" cutter. This will probably be one of the 90 degree rebating cutters having less projection than the cutter it is supposedly balancing. It is most unlikely that such an arrangement will be in static or dynamic balance and my advice is *always* use matching pairs of profile cutters despite anyone's assurance to the contrary.) All instructions given with or engraved onto cutting tools and blocks should, of course,

be noted and complied with. This would include references to the maximum projection of a cutter from its mounting block and also, very importantly, the proportion of the cutter which is actually clamped. As a general rule in this regard, the cutter should have sufficient body length inserted into the block to ensure that the *full* face of the locking wedge is in contact with it. If in doubt, always clarify with the manufacturer any specific recommendations for a particular tool.

Although cutters of this type are available in literally hundreds of different profiles, it may be that the operator occasionally requires a pattern which is not available. Cutter "blanks" are supplied for this purpose. These are of high carbon steel, but for ease of initial shaping where considerable amounts of metal may have to be removed they are often left unhardened. (Your supplier will advise on this.) After shaping, the new cutters will have to be heat treated by the operator if this is the case. The procedure is to grind the required profile on each cutter blank, taking care to provide "relief" for the cutting edges on all facets of supporting bevels (Fig. 63), and then to harden the cutters by heating them to a dull red and quenching them in an oil bath.

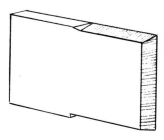

Fig. 63 "Relief" bevels are necessary behind all edges likely to come into contact with the work even if they are not the primary cutting edges. In this example, all waste will be removed by the vertical edge but a slight amount of relief has also been given to the top and bottom edges.

54

The cutting edge can then be given a final sharpening by honing with an oil slip stone. (*Note*: Not all steels can or should be treated in this way. Apart from variations in steel compounds, the design of the tool holder itself may be such that a cutter hardened in this way would break under load – a "French" cutter for example. (See below.) In cases such as this the tool is re-heated after hardening to temper it, that is, to make it less brittle. Professional advice should always be sought, therefore, in relation to any tool requirements or problems.) There are definite safe limits to the amount of stock which can be removed from a cutter before it should be discarded, and foremost amongst these will be the length available for positive clamping. A safe limit for the interchangeable patterns commonly used on circular blocks would be nine tenths of the original length, but no specific recommendations are made at present under U.K. regulations and users should always, therefore, check with the tool manufacturers.

Of perhaps even greater concern is the amount of *projection* from its block at which any cutter may be used. Again, no specific recommendations are made by the Health and Safety Executive, but it is clear that the frequency and severity of accidents occurring at spindle moulders increases directly in relation to increased cutter projection. It should be remembered, of course, that not all moulding blocks offer a projection setting mechanism by which the position of the cutters in relation to the body of the block can be varied. Even so, the *principles* of adopting safely low feed speeds and ensuring that all guards are properly set and of sufficiently strong construction to contain a "flying" cutter, must be adhered to, and a consciousness of the increased stresses which "lengthy" cutter projection imposes, developed.

Very thin grinding wheels are obtainable from most engineers' merchants and can be interchanged with one of the wheels on any double-ended grinder. (Check the diameter and bore size of an existing wheel before going to your supplier:

"... it's a sort of greenish one with the switch on the top ..." isn't really what he needs to know.

A set of shaped files and slip stones are also very useful for profile cutter maintenance (Fig. 64).

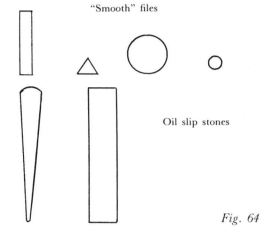

"Smooth" files

Oil slip stones

Fig. 64

"Cutter development" is one of those frustrating but unavoidable intrusions affecting so many seemingly straightforward propositions. It is not enough to simply make a sectional drawing of the cutter profile you require directly from a cross section of timber. The cutter profile has to be elongated or "developed" to take account of its angle of presentation to the work. (Fig. 65.) The geometry of this development can be plotted and for large establishments this is the normal procedure before grinding cutters to produce a particular profile. Some experience and appreciation of cutter development required in any given circumstance can be acquired, however, simply by comparing a timber moulding with the flat profile of the cutter used to produce it. It will be found that as the distance from the central point of rotation increases, so the elongation of the cutter profile has to be increased. Although this development is fractional, it is, nevertheless, important if accurate results are desired.

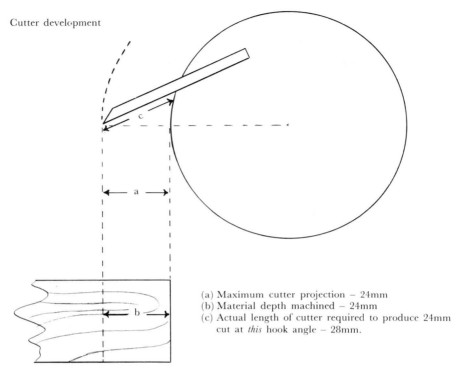

Cutter development

(a) Maximum cutter projection – 24mm
(b) Material depth machined – 24mm
(c) Actual length of cutter required to produce 24mm
   cut at *this* hook angle – 28mm.

Fig. 65 The fixed angle at which the cutters are set in the block (plan view) has a foreshortening effect and the cutter profile must be "developed" (stretched) to take account of this.

Solid Profile Blocks

As the name implies, these tools are purpose-made to produce a particular profile and wherever there is a consistent demand for specific mouldings, this pattern of block provides the most economical means of production. As with block and interchangeable cutter systems, these solid blocks are available in a huge range of profiles for almost every conceivable requirement. Their principal working advantages over other tooling systems are that they will run tens of thousands of metres of timber between services and the inherent accuracy of cutting edge register against a workface means that consistent results are attainable at comparatively high feed rates. The cutting tips of solid profile blocks are usually of high speed steel or tungsten carbide and silver soldered to a block body which matches the tip profile (Fig. 66). Besides providing direct support for the cutting tips, this pattern of body also provides a "chip limiting" effect (see below).

Re-grinding or honing of solid profile blocks is carried out on the *face*, rather than the bevel of the tips. This means that the original balance and profile of blocks is relatively simple to maintain. (Honing with an oil slip stone is an operation which the user can carry out without difficulty, but re-

grinding is best done on a precision grinder so that equal amounts are removed from all tip faces and the balance of the block is preserved.

Fig. 66(a) Solid profile blocks are frequently used in combinations (or stacks) to obtain the desired profile. This example does not incorporate chip limiting protrusions. (Photo: courtesy J.KO. Cutters Ltd., High Wycombe.)

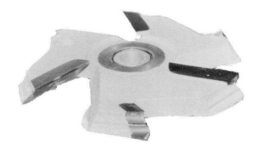

(b) This example of a solid profile block has separate tips (6 in total) for cutting the field-face and shoulder of raised and fielded panels. (Photo: courtesy Omas Tooling, Tiverton.)

(c) The body of this block has been forged to the same profile as the cutting tips to provide chip thickness limitation. (Photo: courtesy Omas Tooling, Tiverton.)

Solid profile blocks can be obtained with four or more cutting tips so that increased feed speeds can be used in the production of regularly required mouldings. (Feed speeds are dictated by cutter "frequency" and diameter). "Frequency" is the term used to describe the number of cuts per minute effected by a cutting tool and this in turn is related to the number of cutting tips and revolutions per minute of the drive shaft. For example, a cutter frequency of 12,000 cuts per minute can be achieved with a two knife cutter-block rotating at 6,000 rpm. A four knife cutter-block could be driven at just 3,000 rpm to achieve the same frequency of 12,000 cuts per minute. Put another way, the four knife block rotating at 6,000 rpm could be fed at twice the speed of the two knife block. Cutter-block diameter is also important as shown in Fig. 67. In small

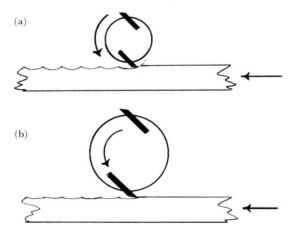

(a)

(b)

Fig. 67 Cutter "frequency" and diameter are significant factors in determining feed speeds which will leave no visible pitch marks. (Pitch marks and frequency have been exaggerated for clarity.)
(a) is a two cutter moulding block rotating at 6000 rpm being fed at 6 metres (20 ft) per minute.
(b) is a larger diameter block rotating and fed at the same speed. Pitch marks in this example are less noticeable due to the larger cutting arc. A similar effect could be achieved by feeding (a) at a slower speed.

workshops, of course, this sort of analysis is largely irrelevant as feed speeds will be adjusted by the operator in line with the surface finish required. When the small workshop is on the threshold of continuous production, however, it is important that the planner be aware of all the factors governing output potential.

French Cutters

This type of moulding cutter is still supplied for some spindle moulders but by its nature must be used with proper caution.

Two factors should be considered. Firstly, it is the flat *face* of the cutting edge which meets the work and care must be taken not to feed the work onto the cutter too fast, otherwise it will be impossible for the actual cutting edge to work the material at all and a kick-back or cutter failure is bound to occur. (Fig. 68.)

(a)

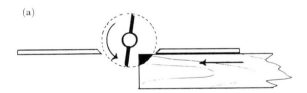

Fig. 68(a) **Wrong!** — *The scraping action of "French" cutters necessitates a slow feed and light cuts to ensure that the work does not meet the flat face of the cutter with consequent cutter-failure and/or material rejection.*

(b)

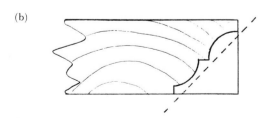

(b) Production of mouldings with **any** *type of cutter can be speeded considerably by removing the bulk of the waste with bench or bandsaw before moulding.*

Secondly, there is no "chip limiting" factor provided by the presence of a supporting tool body and the aperture between in-feed and out-feed fences will consequently be almost entirely open twice during each revolution of the cutter. If used with due regard to these points (i.e. slow feeds in conjunction with light cuts), Fench cutters will give good results, particularly on hardwoods, due to their "scraping" rather than slicing angle of work contact.

Chip Limiters

Although in some countries the authorities specify that hand-fed moulding machines should only be fitted with cylindrical cutter-

(a)

Solid profile block, chip limiting arrangement.

(b)

Block and interchangeable cutters,
chip limiting arrangement.

Fig. 69 Chip limiters can be an integral part of the moulding block (a), or interchangeable to match any particular cutters used (b). They are profiled as the principal cutting edge, but describe a fractionally smaller arc during rotation. The maximum chip that can be removed in a single revolution is limited to this difference in cutting tip and limiter projection.

blocks, current U.K. regulations state that surface planers alone *must* be fitted with this type of block. The advantage of cylindrical blocks from a safety standpoint is that they automatically limit the amount of stock that can be removed by any cutting tip in a single revolution to the equivalent of its projection from the block body. This maximum projection will be much less in the case of cylindrical or circular blocks than

is the case with "square" blocks or "French" cutters.

The principle of chip limiting has been further developed either by manufacturing the cutter-block itself to the same profile as the cutting tip, the system used on solid profile blocks; or, for blocks with interchangeable cutters, by fitting identically profiled blank cutters in front of working cutters as shown in Fig. 69.

Using The Spindle Moulder

The force spent in cutting any workpiece is directional and occurs at a tangent to the arc of the cutting tool at its point of contact with the work. (Fig. 70.) The practical effect of this is that cutting force is not simply directed back along the in-feed fence towards the operator but an element of that force is tending to pull the work into the aperture.

Fig. 70 The "strike", or cutter rejection force resisting feed force, is directed along a tangent to the cutting arc at the point of work contact. The practical difference in control pressure required to ensure an undeviating and safe feed line can be seen by studying the two examples. In (ii), the spread of cutter force is such that for much of its contact time each cutter is trying to pull the work directly into the aperture. Compensatory control pressure will need to be directed through the workpiece onto the fences.

i) Showing the direction and spread of cutter force
   resisting a feed when set up for light cutting

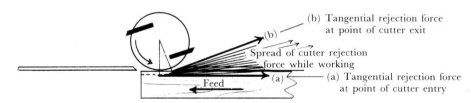

(b) Tangential rejection force
at point of cutter exit

Spread of cutter rejection
force while working

(a) Tangential rejection force
at point of cutter entry

Feed

ii) Showing the direction and spread of
   cutter force resisting a feed when
   set up for heavy cutting

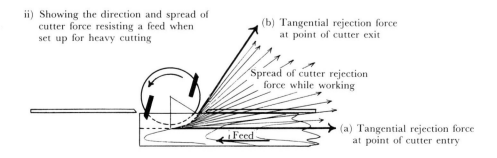

(b) Tangential rejection force
at point of cutter exit

Spread of cutter rejection
force while working

(a) Tangential rejection force
at point of cutter entry

Feed

This must be controlled by pressure against the in-feed fence. As the cut progresses the work receives support from the out-feed fence but of course at some stage of feed the tail-end of the work will leave the in-feed fence and it is at this point that cutter pulling force is at its maximum due to the distance of the nearest support point, (i.e. the nose of the out-feed fence). (Fig. 71.)

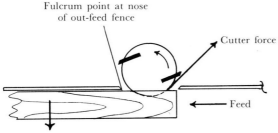

Fulcrum point at nose of out-feed fence

Cutter force

Feed

Work will tend to pivot away from out-feed fence at this stage of the feed unless checked

Fig. 71 The leverage exerted by the cutting force is at its maximum as the tail-end of the workpiece leaves the support of the in-feed fence. Unless adequate control pressure is applied to keep the work in contact with the out-feed fence its tail-end will dip into the aperture and a heavier cut.

For this reason, my own preference for spindle moulder guarding is the type favoured by many continental authorities, namely, a simple aperture guard, adjusted so that the work can just pass below it and manual fence control pressure, or, spring pressure directed against the fences and *not* the aperture as is so often the case with the "Shaw" type guards provided on many machines. (Fig. 72a.) However, this practice cannot be recommended for use in any moulding operations other than those involving wide boards as the cutters must be enclosed as far as is practicable under current U.K. regulations. For narrow workpieces, in any case, the "tunnel" arrangement of a vertical and horizontal pressure guard is preferable (Fig. 72c), as it effectively prevents the work from flexing or chattering away from the cutters.

Fig. 72(a) The hood guard covers the exposed portion of the cutter and deflects chips away from the operator. Horizontal, manual or spring pressure can be used to maintain positive contact with the feed control fences.

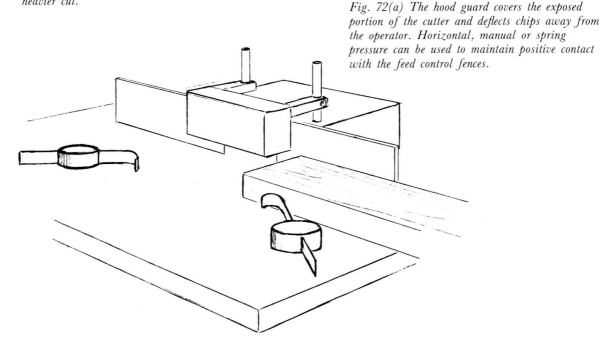

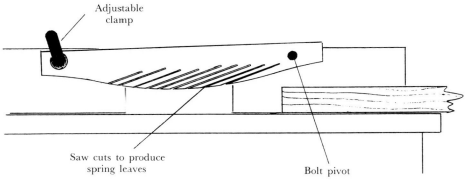

Adjustable
clamp

Saw cuts to produce
spring leaves

Bolt pivot

Fig. 72(b) Downward pressure to prevent chatter under the cutting action can be applied manually if the workpiece is sufficiently large, or mechanically if either hand would otherwise have to pass unacceptably close to the cutter. If a proprietary spring guard is not available a wooden substitute should be made.

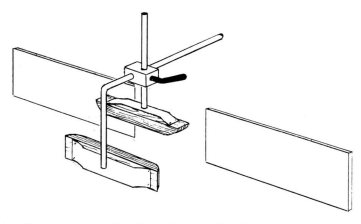

(c) Shaw guards provide adjustable vertical and horizontal spring pressure but care should be taken to ensure that the horizontal pressure shoe is directing its control pressure onto the feed fences and not only the cutter aperture.

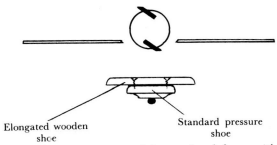

Elongated wooden
shoe

Standard pressure
shoe

*(d) Where large diameter cutters are being used and fences withdrawn accordingly, it may be that the standard pressure shoe is directing **all** its "controlling" force into the aperture. In such cases an elongated shoe should be fixed to the original.*

Downward control pressure onto the table becomes most important in any operation involving a "top cut" as deviation from the horizontal line of the table during feed will result in a heavier cut than planned being taken. Hand-fed moulding operations are, therefore, best carried out with a "bottom" rather than "top" cut, whenever possible. (Fig. 73.) This has the added advantage of reducing the amount of cutter exposed. It may be that some tools are of too large a diameter to be wound down into the table aperture. In this case the operator may find it well worth-while to make a false table from blockboard or similar material that can be clamped to the existing table. A close fitting aperture can then be cut in the false table so that the required bottom cutting tool can be used.

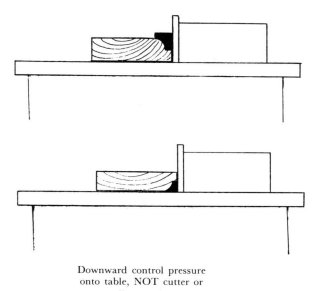

Fig. 73(a) Moulding produced with a top cut. Loss of contact with the table surface through work chatter, or "movement" due to relieved stress, or simple operator error will result in the workpiece moving into a heavier cut than planned.

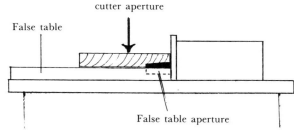

*(b) The same moulding produced with a bottom cut. Any deviation in the feed line from the table will now result in the work moving **out** of cut. This arrangement also has the benefit of reducing the amount of cutter exposed to the minimum essential for any particular mould production.*

Downward control pressure onto table, NOT cutter or cutter aperture

False table

False table aperture

(c) When using a bottom cutter of a larger diameter than the fixed table aperture, a false table can be made and clamped to the fixed table. An aperture to suit the large diameter cutter can now be cut into the false table.

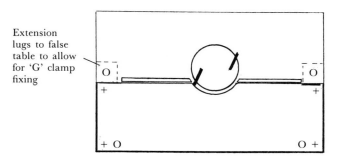

Extension lugs to false table to allow for 'G' clamp fixing

(d) The false table can be bolted to the fixed table if that can be drilled at suitable fixing points around the lip (+).
Alternatively 'G' clamps can be used in positions out of the feed line (O).

End-grain Moulding

It is often the case when moulding end-grain sections that the workpiece receives no support from the feed control fences at all (Fig. 74). It is therefore essential that control during feed of the work across the cutter is provided by other means. This is generally with a horizontal sliding table, fence and work-clamp. As will be seen from Fig. 75(a), two problems arise if the sliding table and fence are used without modification. Firstly, there is no support for the work immediately behind the point of cut and excessive clamping pressure will be needed to hold the work. Secondly, for the same reason, "spelching" (i.e. splintering or break-out) of the grain will occur at the point where the cutter breaks through. Provision of a "spelching fence" attached to the main carriage fence will overcome both these problems. (Fig. 75).

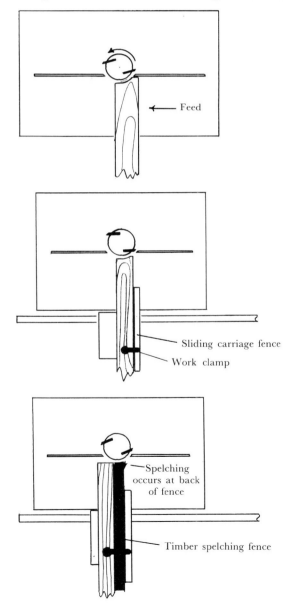

Fig. 74 **Wrong!** *If the fences are to be relied upon for feed control the edge being machined must be at least four times the width of the aperture.*
Particularly in end-grain moulding, the end passing across the cutter may be receiving insufficient or no support at all from the fences and purely manual control must not be attempted.

Fig. 75(a) The sliding carriage with work clamp (also referred to as a tenoning table) provides a suitable means of holding and feeding narrow end-grain sections safely.
In some cases the fence cannot be advanced sufficiently close to the cutting arc to give maximum support to the workpiece and chatter and splelching will occur. (See 75b below)
   Note: Although the split fences do not now play any part in feed control, they have been set to guard the non-working arc of the cutter.

(b) The spelching fence is prepared from timber and fixed to the main carriage fence. It extends onto the table as far as the workpiece itself and is consequently machined in the same way as the feed proceeds. Maximum support is therefore provided exactly where it is needed to prevent spelching as the cutter breaks out of the workpiece.

63

The Through-fence

The main danger in feeding a spindle moulder occurs at the point of cutter/work contact and where the work is largely unsupported. A through fence will provide such support. This fence extends right across the table without any aperture or gap other than that which has been machined away by the cutter itself. The only exposed portion of the cutter is therefore the working part and the workpiece cannot suddenly dip into the aperture through overloading or lack of sufficient fence control pressure. The preparation of a through-fence does, however, involve a "dropping on" operation which must be understood and controlled.

The new fence is made by machining a board to the approximate thickness and other combined dimensions of the two existing fences at their furthest point apart (Fig. 76). The chosen cutter is then mounted on the spindle and *raised* to the required height above the table. (*Raising* any vertically adjustable cutterhead will take up back-lash in the adjusting mechanism and obviate any possibility of the head dropping in use. Similarly, any geared fence or table adjustment should be made with the adjuster *pushing* the component to the required setting.)

There are three ways of fixing the new fence as shown in Fig. 77. The important point in using either method is ensure that the operation is perfectly controlled with the use of stops. When using either method of through-fence preparation, it is as well to limit the drop-on travel to about 12 mm ($\frac{1}{2}$"). If a final cutter projection of say 25 mm (1") is required, this can then be achieved in successive drop-on procedures of 12 mm ($\frac{1}{2}$"), switching off the machine each time adjustments to stops are made. Limiting the possible distance that the through-fence can travel in this way will give the operator experience in controlling the snatch of the cutter as it tries to pull the fence onto itself.

In cases where a through-fence is desirable for safety but a complete face moulding is required, then a packing piece of suitable thickness will have to be fixed to the out-feed side of the fence. The thickness of the packing piece can be established by feeding a test piece over the cutter in the conventional way and withdrawing it after a few millimetres have been machined. With the machine switched off, the test piece can be repositioned and the gap between the machined face and the out-feed portion of the fence measured. It is then a simple matter to thickness an appropriate packing piece and screw or clamp it to the through-fence (Fig. 78.)

Once the operator has had experience of working with a through-fence on a spindle moulder it is certain he will always favour this method of working where feasible.

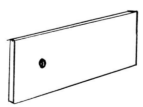
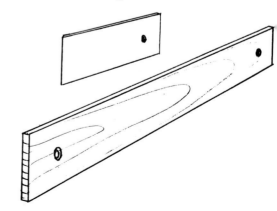

Fig. 76 The "through-fence" can be prepared from timber thicknessed to about 10mm ($\frac{3}{8}$") and cut to the overall dimensions of the existing split fences. Countersunk holes allow for bolting or screwing the new fence in position against the split fences or alternatively 'G' clamps can be used above the feed line.

64

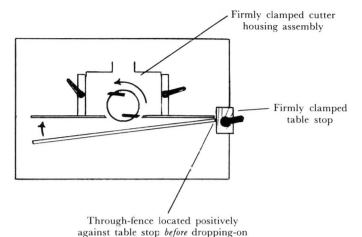

Firmly clamped cutter
housing assembly

Firmly clamped
table stop

Through-fence located positively
against table stop *before* dropping-on
to rotating cutter

Fig. 77(a) Preparation of a through-fence for fixing to existing split fences. After the cutter has been used to cut its own aperture in the new fence, the fence is hinged away from the cutter, taking care to keep the right-hand end in position against the table stop until clear of the cutter-block. The machine is then switched off before screwing, bolting or clamping the new fence in its working position.

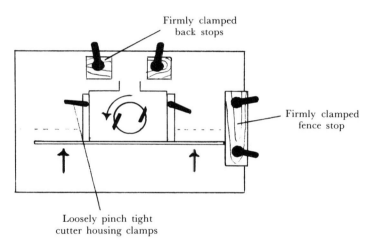

Firmly clamped
back stops

Firmly clamped
fence stop

Loosely pinch tight
cutter housing clamps

(b) Preparation of a through-fence which replaces the split fences. With the through-fence fixed to the cutter housing assembly and the cutter housing clamps screwed down so that horizontal movement is still just possible, the whole assembly is slowly pushed back onto the rotating cutter-block.

The back stops provide positive location in the desired working position and the fence stop absorbs and checks any kick or chatter due to excess clearance in the assembly clamping slots.

Immediately the assembly is in its final position the cutter housing clamps are fully tightened.

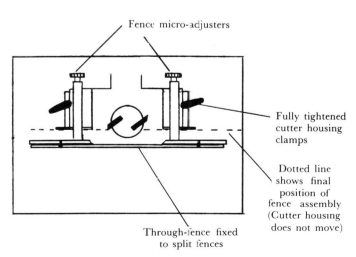

Fence micro-adjusters

Fully tightened
cutter housing
clamps

Dotted line
shows final
position of
fence assembly
(Cutter housing
does not move)

Through-fence fixed
to split fences

(c) If the spindle moulder is fitted with micro-adjusting fences, the through-fence can be fixed to the split fences and pulled back onto the rotating cutter by simultaneous adjustment of the micro-setting controls. The housing/fence assembly must be firmly clamped to the table for this operation. (It may be necessary to undertake this procedure in two stages to achieve the required depth of fence penetration.)

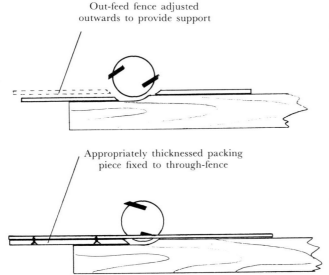

Out-feed fence adjusted
outwards to provide support

Appropriately thicknessed packing
piece fixed to through-fence

Fig. 78(a) In a moulding operation where the full height of the edge is being machined, the out-feed fence is adjusted to take up the gap.

*   **Note**: This fence adjustment is always made with the machine switched off.*

(b) If the out-feed fence cannot be adjusted independently of the in-fence for any reason (such as the use of a through-fence), then a packing piece must be fixed to the fence on the out-feed side of the cutter if a gap between the fence and workpiece would otherwise occur.

The Ring Fence

It is sometimes necessary to machine mouldings on irregularly shaped edges. The conventional straight fences cannot be used under these circumstances and a device called the ring fence is substituted. This is a circular fence which is concentric with the cutter-block and of a slightly smaller diameter than the cutter arc. The ring fence may take the form of a stepped table aperture insert or, preferably, a ball-bearing ring which is mounted on the spindle itself either above or below the cutter-block. Collars of different diameters can be fitted over the ball-bearing to vary the amount of cutter projection (Fig. 79).

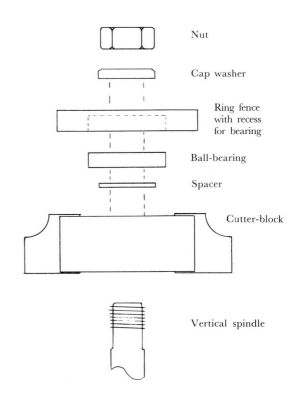

Nut

Cap washer

Ring fence
with recess
for bearing

Ball-bearing

Spacer

Cutter-block

Vertical spindle

Fig. 79 (right) Cutter projection beyond the diameter of the ring fence can be varied either by using a moulding block which incorporates a cutter projection adjustment, or by interchanging the ring-fence itself for one of a larger or smaller diameter.

If a template is not being used it is important that the work-face itself is finished to the required standard before moulding as irregularities in the face will be reproduced in the moulding. Of course, the moulding of an entire face cannot be carried out by this method as one part of the face is necessarily in contact with the ring fence (Fig. 80.)

Fig. 80(a) Initially, the work is pushed onto (or led onto) the cutter-block/ring fence assembly. It will be seen that the cutters machine away the waste to produce the required moulding only until further advance onto rotating cutters is checked by the ring fence. Feed then continues **along** *the table to produce the mould along the entire edge. This initial contact with the cutter-block must be controlled to prevent a kick back – see (b) and (c) below.*

Note: *REGULATIONS REQUIRE THAT A JIG OR WORK HOLDER WITH HANDLES IS USED FOR THIS TYPE OF WORK WHEREVER PRACTICABLE.*

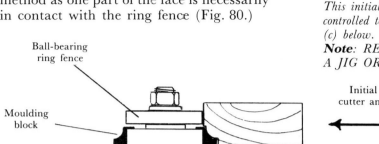

Ball-bearing ring fence

Moulding block

Initial feed onto cutter and ring fence

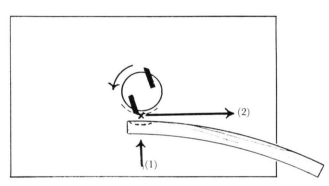

(b) **Wrong!** *If the workpiece is "dropped on" to the cutter (1) in this manner and without the use of a clamped table stop to prevent any possibility of the work moving with cutter rotation, the resulting heavy cut and kick-back may result in total material rejection (2).*

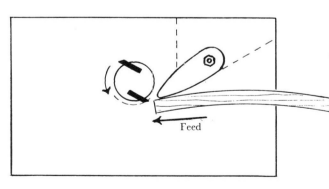

Feed

(c) To achieve a progressive and fully controlled entry onto the cutter without the conventional in-feed fence a "finger fence" can be made and bolted in the position shown. The finger fence must be absolutely immoveable once fixed and if there is any doubt about this it can be made, as shown by the dotted lines, to extend to the table edge where it can be clamped.

It may sometimes be feasible to use the conventional in-feed fence for running-on to the cutter-block and this has the advantage that the cutter guard/housing can be left in position.

Should a full edge moulding be required then a template will have to be made.

This is, in fact, the best way to use a ring fence as it is the *template* which is prepared to a perfect finish and successive workpieces can be rough sawn to a slightly larger dimension (so that they overhang the template by a fraction) and attached to the template. Now, of course, it is the edge of the template which makes contact with the ring fence and this controls the depth of moulding produced on the workpiece (Fig. 81). A further advantage in using a template is that it can be extended horizontally beyond the nose and tail of the work to provide "lead-in" and "lead-out" control. The work does not then have to be "dropped-on" to the cutter (Fig. 82). The extension of the template in this way, also provides a convenient platform for work holding clamps.

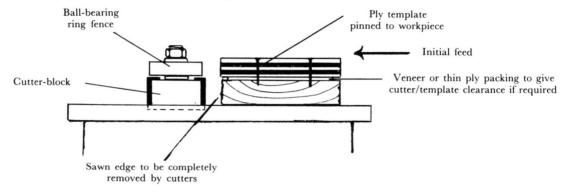

Ball-bearing ring fence

Ply template pinned to workpiece

Initial feed

Cutter-block

Veneer or thin ply packing to give cutter/template clearance if required

Sawn edge to be completely removed by cutters

Fig. 81 The simplest form of ring fence moulding with a template. Once the template has been prepared, successive workpieces can be rough sawn to about 3mm ($\frac{1}{8}$") full (oversize) and machined to the exact template profile with either a 90°, clean edge or any selected section profile.

In preparing the template, due allowance must be made for the projection of the cutters beyond the ring fence or otherwise. In the illustration above, for example, the finished workpiece will be slightly smaller than the template.

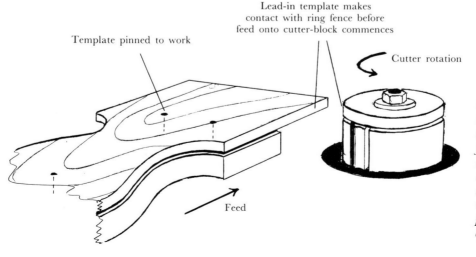

Lead-in template makes contact with ring fence before feed onto cutter-block commences

Template pinned to work

Cutter rotation

Feed

Fig. 82(a) Extending the nose and tail of a template. As forward feed commences the cutters will remove only a small and controlled amount of waste in each revolution (directly proportional to the rate of forward feed).

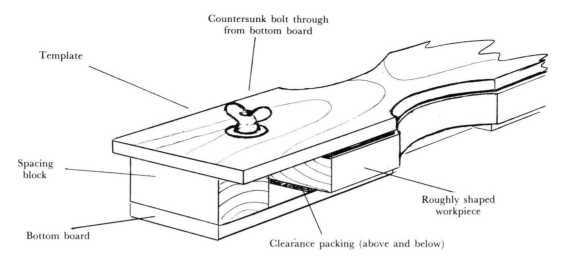

Countersunk bolt through from bottom board

Template

Spacing block

Bottom board

Roughly shaped workpiece

Clearance packing (above and below)

(b) Extension of the template nose and tail has the additional benefit of providing a platform for a work clamping arrangement.

The jig shown illustrates a simple "sandwich" principle and could easily be modified to include handles, single action clamps and workpiece positioning stops, if the production demand is substantial.

The extra weight and stability given to workpieces by jig mounting also contributes a great deal to general safety.

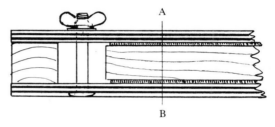

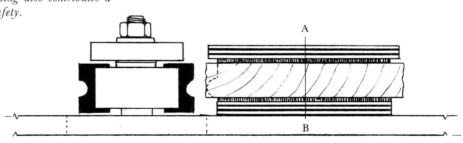

The main restriction in ring fence moulding is one of guarding the operation to standards which would be acceptable under Health & Safety regulations. It seems doubtful that this is actually possible at all as the sides of the cutter-block need to be exposed when moulding concave profiles. Certainly, a top guard must be used and the operator should at all times be conscious that his fingers are not overhanging the front edge of the workpiece. Very often in ring fencing the work is swung around during the progress of a feed to use a different part of the cutter-block and a finger that was a safe distance from the block can be at great risk without the operator even being aware of it. Because of this I consider it essential for the operator's own safety and peace of mind to adopt as standard practice the use of proper work-holding jigs with handles in any moulding operation involving the use of a ring fence. This is, in fact, a requirement of current U.K. legislation.

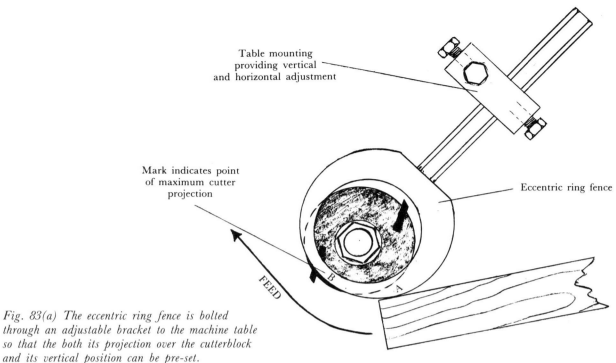

Table mounting
providing vertical
and horizontal adjustment

Mark indicates point
of maximum cutter
projection

Eccentric ring fence

FEED

B

A

Fig. 83(a) The eccentric ring fence is bolted
through an adjustable bracket to the machine table
so that the both its projection over the cutterblock
and its vertical position can be pre-set.

By placing the workpiece on the table and
against the eccentric fence in position "A" it is in
contact with all the necessary feed control surfaces
before it contacts the cutters. Progressive feed to
position "B" will bring the workpiece safely and
predictably into the full cut.

(b) Setting the eccentric ring fence
projection over the cutters to vary the
depth of cut. In use the top and sides
of the assembly will be shrouded by
an adjustable bonnet guard. (Photo:
courtesy Startrite Ltd.,
Gillingham, Kent.)

A bonnet guard is available from most manufacturers to be used during operations such as those described in this section. This has a close mesh, cage top and adjustable side flanges which can be lowered to cover the sides and back of the cutter-block assembly. It should be accepted that this type of guard is not only an essential requirement under law before ring fencing is carried out but that even where the law may not apply, it is most definitely a requirement for any operator's safety.

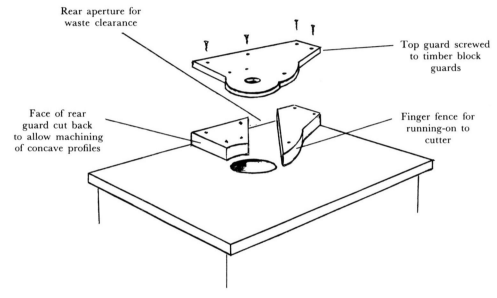

Rear aperture for waste clearance

Top guard screwed to timber block guards

Face of rear guard cut back to allow machining of concave profiles

Finger fence for running-on to cutter

Fig. 84 Very few machines are supplied with satisfactory guards for ring fencing and the operator must always ensure that appropriate guards are made and fitted to cover all nonworking sections of the cutter arc.

This simple timber and multi-ply guard can be tailored to suit the job in hand and clamped or bolted in position.

Back Fencing

There are occasions in some joinery shops when the spindle moulder is used with a back fence rather than the conventional split, or through fences. As a hand-fed operation this is hazardous in the extreme since any deviation from the line of feed will result in an immediate and uncontrollable deepening of the cut with consequent kick-back or material break-up. The operation can, however, be very useful if power feed is available. It will be seen from Fig. 85 that back fencing is a combined thicknessing/edge moulding operation which can be used for reducing the width of sections that are too wide to be handled in the normal way with a thicknesser. (Doors and wide panel constructions for example.) In some instances an edge moulding is incorporated as in the case of "nosing" stair treads or preparing tongue-and-groove boards. As with all feeding operations, but more so, the operator should stand a little to one side of the potential rejection path. For reasons explained above, the force with which material may be rejected from a "trapped" state is very considerable indeed.

Probably the most useful adaptation of back fencing in a workshop without power feed conversion units for independent machines, such as the spindle moulder, is with a drum sander. Work which is too small to be finished or finely dimensioned in any other way can be fed between a sanding drum and back fence to produce an exact dimension and face finish. (NOTE: Even though there are no rotating or linear cutters to be considered in this operation, care must, nevertheless, be taken to keep fingers away from abrasive surfaces *and* the workpiece must be fed in the correct way, that is, *against* the direction of the drum rotation and with the use of push sticks if necessary.)

FINALLY, RE-READ THE TEN GENERAL RULES FOR SAFE WOOD-MACHINING IN CHAPTER ONE.

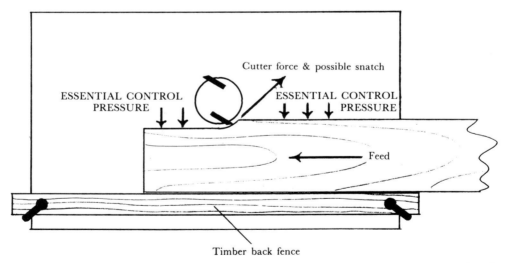

Fig. 85 It will be seen from this diagram of the forces involved in "back fence" moulding that the slightest deviation in feed line away from the back fence will result in a deepening cut and snatch with consequent kick-back. A power feed unit could be well utilized to provide safe feed and control pressure.

*   **Note**: *The **only** safe method of back fencing is with the aid of mechanical, not manual, control pressure. Also, of course, as with all machining operations, the non-working part of the cutter must be properly guarded.*

CHAPTER FIVE

The Bandsaw

The remarkable usefulness of the narrow bandsaw is not generally appreciated by those woodmachinists entering the small workshop scene from a heavier industrial woodworking background. In large establishments it will be the case that a purpose-built machine is available for each required function. Small businesses are unlikely to have either the space or work justification for such an investment and it is here that the narrow bandsaw comes into its own. It has, with good reason in my opinion, been described by some traditional woodworkers as the machine they would least like to be without. This opinion does, however, depend very much on the operator's understanding of the machine and the inherent capacity of the particular machine itself to be properly set-up. A badly designed or commissioned bandsaw will be expensive to run (in terms of replacement blades), and will seem to have a mind of its own, following the line of least resistance when cutting in defiance of fences or threats from its owner.

"Narrow" bandsaws are those with a blade width 75 mm (3") or less. This may seem like anything but a "narrow" blade when compared with the lightweight machines with which we are most familiar and which are usually fitted with blades of up to about 12 mm ($\frac{1}{2}$") in width. The description is more meaningful when considered in the context of other bandsaws such as power-fed band mill-saws and band re-saws. These are often fitted with blades of 200 mm (8") in width or even more. They are used for deep cutting and general high speed timber conversion with a minimum of waste. Narrow bandsaws are used freehand and share little in common with their larger relatives other than a general principle of construction.

Knowledge of certain factors will be helpful in choosing a suitable machine. The blade runs around two or, occasionally, three wheels, one of which is motor driven. For directional stability and accuracy of cut the relationship between the upper and lower wheels is of prime importance. This relationship is controlled by the frame of the machine and particularly the strength of the neck (Fig. 88). Weakness at this point will allow a degree of independent movement between upper and lower wheels and this in turn will adversely affect machine performance. On a bandsaw designed for conversion of timber up to 150 mm (6"), it should not be possible to push or pull the upper frame whilst holding the lower part of the frame and detect movement. In general then, a heavy and rigid frame is most desirable in any machine of this type which will be required to perform at or near its theoretical maximum in cut and loading. Heavy bandwheels will also be an advantage when working near the limits of machine energy output as the flywheel effect and momentum of the rotating parts will give the operator warning of overload

Fig. 86 A good quality floorstanding bandsaw. Note the heavy neck section which contributes to a stable relationship between the top and bottom wheels, (Photo: courtesy Luna Tools & Machinery, Milton Keynes.)

Fig. 87

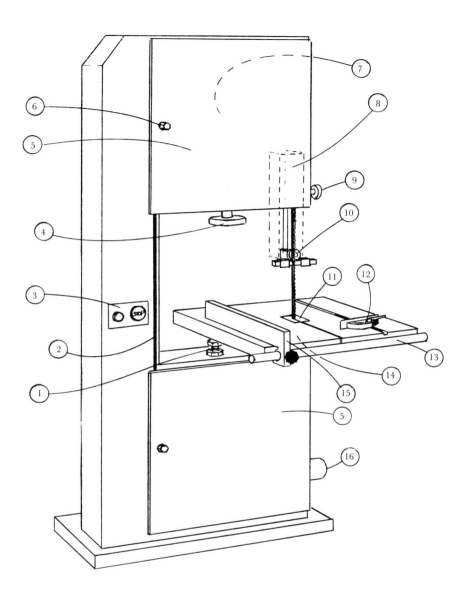

1 Adjustable 90° table stop
2 Blade removal slot (only on "solid" neck machines)
3 ON/OFF switch (also: push button starter)
4 Blade tension adjuster (sometimes on top of upper wheel)
5 Hinged wheel cover (must be locked when machine connected)
6 Cover locking nut   7 Tracking adjustment (at rear of top wheel)
8 Telescopic blade guard (must enclose blade above guides)
9 Thrust/guide assembly vertical setting clamp   10 Thrust/guide assembly
11 Table insert   12 Mitre slide (also: protractor fence or mitre fence)
13 Fence bar   14 Table tilt mechanism and under-table guides
15 Rip fence (also: parallel fence)   16 Extraction duct (also: waste outlet)

before a sudden jam or snatch can occur. In the case of lightweight machines there is far less time for the operator to ease feed pressure in these circumstances, and a jam may often kink or break an otherwise serviceable blade.

At the outset, newcomers to this machine will be happier in accepting that the surface finish obtained from a bandsaw cut *will* require improvement by other methods in the case of face timbers. As with circular sawbenches, therefore, it is more practical to aim for *efficiency* in timber conversion rather than engage in a quest for perfection which realistically is unattainable. The bandsaw is not that sort of machine. What it does offer is immediate access to a deep and comparatively waste-free cutting facility for general timber dimensioning. Even a modestly priced two wheel bandsaw can, for example, handle work of up to 150 mm (6″) in thickness. A circular sawbench to do the same job would, at the time of writing, cost approximately four times the amount. This scope for deep cutting is invaluable in operations such as tenoning when the cost of a purpose-built tennoner cannot be justified. The narrow bandsaw is also the only machine really suited for the shaping operations often called for in furniture construction and the hundred-and-one trimming and blocking jobs that crop up in every wood workshop. Lastly, such a machine is really an essential piece of equipment for woodturners and woodcarvers.

Blade Choice

With the acquisition of any new machine there is always a temptation to buy cutting tools and accessories for every conceivable application. These may or may not prove useful over a long period of time, but, in the main, for every day use, the machine will be fitted with a single general purpose blade. In fact it will be found most inconvenient to change blades for anything other than the

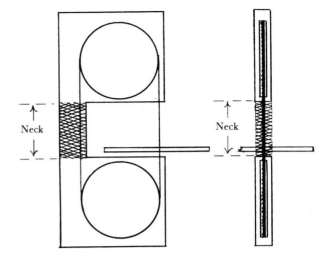

Fig. 88 Strength and rigidity in the neck area of the bandsaw is a pointer to satisfactory cutting performance. If the neck is weak, distortion in the relation between top and bottom bandwheels will prevent correct tensioning and tracking of the blade.

most specialised and demanding of cutting operations (thin, brittle laminates that must be cut without chipping, etc.), and the user will quickly settle into the habit of using blades until they are worn-out and break through fatigue.

In choosing a single blade, therefore, several factors should be considered. Firstly, the type of blade material. It used to be the case that blades fitted to many machines were of the type that could be re-set and sharpened. This had definite disadvantages in the case of very narrow blades in that they had to be "tracked" (see Blade Tracking below) with the teeth overhanging the front edge of the bandwheel to avoid spoiling the set of the inside teeth through compression against the rubber or cork tyre. It was also discovered by users that the cost of re-setting and re-sharpening a narrow bandsaw blade of 19 mm ($\frac{3}{4}$″) or less was more or less the same as the replacement cost. Consequently, the blades now most widely favoured are those of the disposable type which are of the same steel used for many metal cutting applications, (although with a different tooth pitch and configuration and at a lower speed than the optimum for wood cutting). The hardness of these blades is such that they cannot be re-set as the teeth will break rather than bend. They also have a much longer service life than the softer steel types and of course can be used for cutting abrasive materials such as plastic laminates and resin bonded particle boards. The back, or main body, of the blade is tempered to draw some of the hardness from it so that it can flex around the periphery of the bandwheels without prematurely fatiguing. Such blades are designated "hardened and tempered back". They are generally recognizable because of a blue colouration resulting from oxidization during tempering.

Having decided on blade material, blade width and pitch must be considered. At the point where the blade meets the work it is essentially a thin, unsupported ribbon of steel. Tensioning, or stretching, the blade over the bandwheels is therefore necessary if it is to cut accurately. It follows that a wide bodied blade, say 19 mm ($\frac{3}{4}''$) as opposed to 6 mm ($\frac{1}{4}''$), will hold a better line than a thinner one due to its resistance to flexing in the kerf (Fig. 89). Narrow bandsaws,

however, are generally fitted with motors which are *adequate* but with little or no surplus of power. In other words, provided blade choice and all other factors of commissioning are taken account of, the bandsaw will cut to its theoretical maximum. For reasons explained below a wide blade may well limit the bandsaw's overall performance and usefulness.

The theoretical width and pitch of a blade selected for deep tenon cutting would be determined by the nature of the proposed task, i.e. a wide body for good directional stability as the blade will only be required to cut in straight lines, and, a coarse tooth pitch for waste carrying and minimum loss of energy through friction. In practice, several other factors become evident. Firstly, a proportion of the waste produced in cutting falls below the level of the work table and is compressed between the wheel and blade.

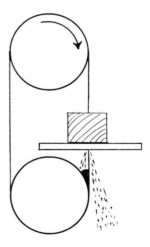

Fig. 90 Waste trapped and compressed between the blade and bandwheel below the table.

An accumulation of resin dust therefore builds up predominantly on one face of the blade, spoiling clearance and eventually causing the blade to adopt a slight directional bias as it tries to equalize available clearance between both its faces in the kerf. Further, because there is little or no *reserve* of power, the increased frictional

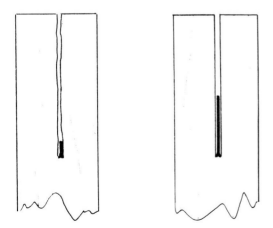

Fig. 89 A wide bodied blade will hold a better line than a narrow one due to its greater rigidity and resistance to flexing in the kerf.

resistance limits deep cutting potential as available energy is increasingly directed to overcoming drag rather than cutting. Reducing the blade width will automatically reduce the area on which a resin build-up can occur and cutting performance will be found to be more consistent during the life of the blade.

Another limitation imposed by the choice of a wide bodied blade is its inability to cope with tight radius cutting. A 19 mm ($\frac{3}{4}''$) blade, for example, will be hard pressed to cut a circle of 300 mm (12″) in diameter, whereas a 9 mm ($\frac{3}{8}''$) blade will easily cut 50 mm (2″) diameter circle. All things considered I have found that a 300 mm (12″) throat, 150 mm (6″) cut, narrow bandsaw is at its most useful for general conversion and shaping work when fitted with a 9 mm ($\frac{3}{8}''$), 4 or 6 teeth per inch blade.

Blade Changing

A question asked by many woodworkers not thoroughly familiar with the narrow bandsaw is, "What happens when a blade breaks?" (Visions of the blade leaving the machine at high speed prompt the question and I suspect that the real question is, "In which direction should I throw myself when a blade breaks?") In fact, provided the machine is properly guarded, nothing happens which can possibly cause injury to the operator. The "bang!" which is heard is caused by the spring tension of the upper bandwheel being suddenly released. As the blade breaks, it immediately loses the necessary contact with the motor driven bandwheel and, having virtually no mass and consequent momentive energy of its own, stops at once. In the case of a bandsaw, as with most other woodworking machines, "proper guarding" means guarding which covers every part of the cutting tool other than that part which is necessarily exposed to cut the material being worked.

(Larger bandsaws and bandsaws using blades of a width greater than say, 25 mm (1″), should be checked periodically for longitudinal blade cracks as this may result in a blade "shredding", without snapping straight across as invariably happens with narrower blades. In such cases, considerable damage may occur if the machine continues running. Also, of course, band re-saw blades and mill saws are very much heavier than the 6 mm–12 mm ($\frac{1}{4}''$–$\frac{1}{2}''$) wide blades generally found on small bandsaws, and consequently store vastly more energy when in motion.)

When changing or fitting a blade, the first check should be to ensure that the teeth of the descending part of the blade are pointing downwards. If the blade appears to have been welded "the wrong way", simply turn it inside-out. (I know of one customer who drove forty furious miles to his supplier to discover this procedure.) With the replacement blade loosely positioned over the bandwheels, the blade guide/thrust assemblies above and below the table must be withdrawn so that they do not interfere with the next operations of "tensioning" and "tracking".

Blade Tensioning

Tensioning, or more correctly perhaps, "straining" the bandsaw blade is essential both for the transmission of drive power and its predictable cutting performance. This is done by raising the top wheel until the blade is sufficiently taut. Judging the correct degree of tension is very much a matter of experience. If the blade is insufficiently stretched it will wander into the line of least resistance when cutting, particularly rip-cutting. If the blade is over-tensioned, there will be unnecessary strain on the blade itself and, in the case of lightweight machines, possible distortion of the machine frame in the region of the neck which controls the relationship between the top and bottom wheels.

Experience in tensioning can be gained by observation of blade performance under a variety of tension settings or by leaning on the advice of others who have used an identical machine. Check, and develop a "feel" for blade tension by holding the unsupported part of the blade between thumb and forefinger and moving it from side to side under moderate pressure. I have found that on a 300 mm (12″) throat, 150 mm (6″) cut bandsaw a total lateral movement of between 6 mm (¼″) and 9 mm (⅜″) is a good starting point. (Fig. 91.)

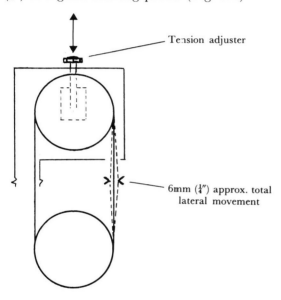

Tension adjuster

6mm (¼″) approx. total lateral movement

Fig. 91 Whilst raising or lowering the upper wheel with the tension adjuster, side to side movement in the unsupported part of the blade is checked under "moderate" thumb and forefinger pressure.

Blade Tracking

"Tracking" is the term used to describe the circumferential running position of the blade in relation to the width of the wheels. In nearly all instances, manufacturers' instructions insist that the blade be particularly tracked so that the teeth of the blade overhang the front edge of the bandwheels with the body of the blade running on the tyres. (Tyres are the rubber or cork bands which are glued to the wheels.) This is not to protect the tyres themselves, which rarely, if ever, need replacement, but rather to prevent the compression of the blade under tension from spoiling the tooth set on the inside or running face of the band. With the introduction of the "hardened" type of blade material for wood cutting, however, (recognizable by the blue colour), this will not be a problem as the teeth are so hard that they will break before bending. The older, conventional, silver-coloured blades were much softer and therefore had to be tracked according to instructions but, even so, this created huge difficulties when working with narrow blades, say 6 mm (¼″), where half the blade width was occupied by the teeth themselves and the operator was left endeavouring to hang a 3 mm (⅛″) ribbon of steel on the forward edge of the wheels.

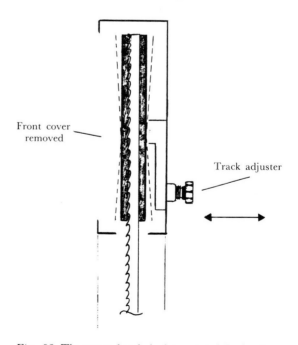

Front cover removed

Track adjuster

Fig. 92 The upper bandwheel is rotated by hand whilst the track adjuster is screwed in or out until the blade adopts a centrally aligned running position.

79

The slightest withdrawal pressure on the back of the blade when backing out of a cut would result in the blade being pulled off the wheels with likely kinking or breakage.

Tracking is carried out by tilting the top wheel in either direction from the vertical whilst rotating the wheel by hand. The tilt adjustment knob is generally situated at the back, (or out-feed side) of the top wheel. My advice, from every point of view, would be to track the blade so that it runs centrally on the bandwheels – provided, of course, that blades of the hardened type are being used. (Fig. 92.)

Thrust Bearing And Guide Block Adjustment

During the tensioning and blade tracking procedures the blade thrust/guide assemblies above and below the table will have been withdrawn so as not to interfere with the free running of the blade. The principle to be understood in setting the guide and thrust components of the bandsaw is that they should at no time interfere with, or check, the free running of the blade. The guide/thrust assemblies are there to support and maintain the pre-set blade attitude. (Fig. 93.)

Thrust bearings or surfaces may be of different types but their function is the same – that is, to prevent the blade being pushed back, and possibly off the bandwheels when material is being fed against the cutting edge of the blade. They should, therefore, be set *just* behind the blade, above and below the table, so that they are clear when the machine is free running but close enough to the blade to check any detectable backwards movement when feed load is applied. They should not be positioned so as to push and distort free line running. This should be checked when setting the thrust surfaces by hand rotation of the upper bandwheel. (All checks and adjustments of this nature should be carried out with the machine

disconnected from the mains supply. It is a logically inexplicable fact that "WET PAINT" signs invite an inquiring finger. ON/OFF switches have the same effect on the motor nerves of many of us and the worst experience I have ever had with a narrow bandsaw was on an occasion when I was checking blade tension and my partner decided, for safety reasons, to check that the machine was disconnected from the mains. He did this by switching the machine on. After the event I could not question the purity of his motives as he was obviously in a worse state of shock than I. The lesson, however, had been learned – **The responsibility of ensuring machine safety lies with the operator**.) This could be classed as a general rule but I don't feel it's necessary to make it additional to the ten in Chapter One.

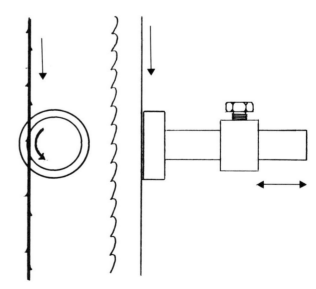

Fig. 93 The thrust bearings above and below the table are brought up behind the blade with minimal clearance so as not to interfere with free running, but close enough to prevent significant backwards movement of the blade as it begins cutting.

Having brought up and locked the thrust bearings, the guide blocks can now be positioned on both sides of the blade above and below the work support table. These give lateral support to the blade body and help to prevent it from twisting under biased feed load. As with thrust bearing positioning, the guide blocks should be just clear of the blade body when the machine is free running. The blocks should be set so that they give maximum support to the body of the blade immediately *behind* the teeth on both sides. (Fig. 94.)

Fig. 94 The guide block carriers above and below the table are adjusted backwards or forwards so that the guide blocks will be positioned just behind the teeth when finally set. Minimal clearance is again provided so that the blocks do not interfere with the free-running of the blade.

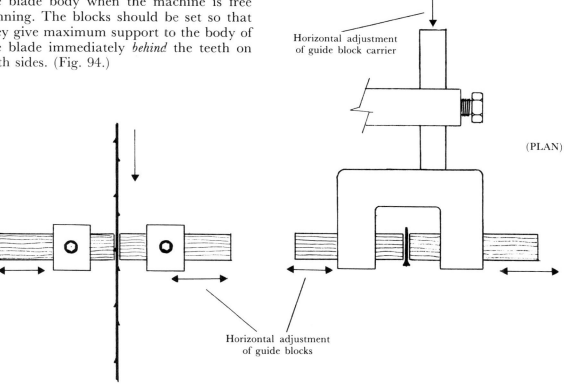

Horizontal adjustment of guide block carrier

(PLAN)

Horizontal adjustment of guide blocks

The guide blocks that are supplied and fitted as standard on most lightweight machines are of a plastic composition and tend to wear or melt under load very quickly. Users will certainly find that the time and small effort required to make hardwood replacements for the original plastic will be well worthwhile.

Brass guide blocks can be made, but I have found that the end grain bearing characteristics of timber (hardwood) are almost as effective and of course much simpler for the woodworker to make and keep in good order. If lignum vitae is available, then blocks made from this species will give exceptional service. (Stern gland bearings for ships' propellers are made from this timber as no metal seems able to match its particular properties of density, strength and self-lubrication.) Other oily hardwoods can be used, such as teak or iroko, or alternatively, any dense bodied timber such as beech. If the timber is of this latter type then soaking it in a light penetrating oil for a few hours before fitting will improve its bearing performance and resistance to wear.

Using The Bandsaw

The operator will quickly discover whether or not the use of fences on his particular machine is feasible. If the machine frame is weak and it has not been possible to tension the blade to its optimum without distorting the frame, then it is highly improbable that the blade will retain directional stability under anything but the lightest of feed loads. In other words, as work is fed along a fence and onto the blade, the cut will deviate from the intended line and either compression of the work between blade and fence will occur or it will be impossible to keep the work in contact with the fence. In either case the blade will be subjected to lateral loads that it was not designed to cope with and will jam or break if feed pressure is maintained. It is far better under such circumstances to use the machine "free-hand" and saw to a pencilled line. In this way any compensatory adjustment can be made much more accurately and a predictable performance assured. (On thin materials or under light feed loads even a blade with considerable lateral bias or "lead" can be made to saw to a fence but the finished cut will be ragged by comparison with a cut obtained from a

properly commissioned machine.)

Unlike the forces experienced when using machines with rotating cutters, the bandsaw's cutting force is always directed downwards and onto the table. It is therefore a pleasant and undemanding machine to use with very few special safety considerations other than those which fall into the category of common sense. Even so, no machine should be approached in a casual or careless way. It is good practice to use a push-stick for the final part of any cut where the fingers would otherwise have to pass dangerously close to the blade. A push-stick is also a very handy implement for removing accumulated offcuts from the machine table. (Do not get into the habit of brushing offcuts away with your hands or fingers.)

It is also important to ensure that work is always supported directly below the point of contact with the blade. In cross cutting cylindrical work, for example, the work will tend to roll in sympathy with the blade force. If this is allowed to happen the operator's hands may be brought into contact with the blade. A work supporting jig such as a V block should be used in such cases. (Fig. 95.)

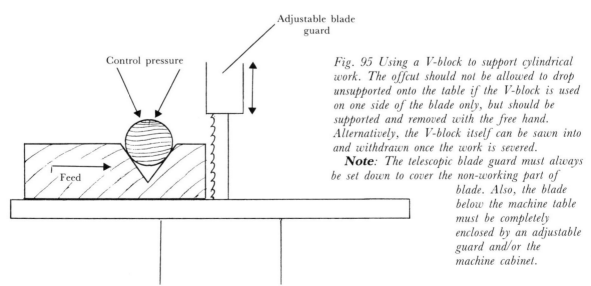

Fig. 95 Using a V-block to support cylindrical work. The offcut should not be allowed to drop unsupported onto the table if the V-block is used on one side of the blade only, but should be supported and removed with the free hand. Alternatively, the V-block itself can be sawn into and withdrawn once the work is severed.

Note: The telescopic blade guard must always be set down to cover the non-working part of blade. Also, the blade below the machine table must be completely enclosed by an adjustable guard and/or the machine cabinet.

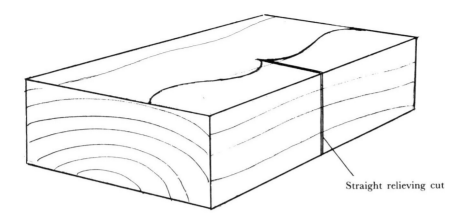

Straight relieving cut

The narrow bandsaw can be an unnecessarily expensive machine to run if care is not taken with cut planning so that blades are not subjected to stresses with which they are not designed to cope. For example, it may sometimes be necessary to back out of cuts, and if the withdrawal is out of a tightly curved cut then pressure on the back of the blade may push it off the front of the bandwheels. The blade is highly likely to be damaged or broken under these circumstances and the simple way to avoid this occurrence is to first make relieving cuts to any point where the blade would otherwise be trapped. (Fig. 96.)

Another cause of premature blade breakage is through the application of excessive lateral pressure. This generally occurs when the operator tries to negotiate tight curves (possibly to avoid backing out of a long curved cut), and tends to twist the feed without maintaining forward feed pressure. This results in the blade itself twisting between the guides and being weakened or permanently distorted if the lateral pressure is such that it actually causes a sudden jam.

A little thought before undertaking any cutting operation with the aim of reducing or doing away with side or back loadings will be well repaid in increased blade life.

Fig. 96 When cutting any contour which may involve backing out of a curved cut it is good practice to make relieving cuts into the problem corners, etc. The blade will then automatically be freed during shaping as it meets any relieving cut and produces an offcut.

CHAPTER SIX

The Radial Arm Saw

The radial arm saw was conceived primarily as a means of overcoming the problems associated with crosscutting long or heavy timbers on a conventional sawbench. In industry it is referred to as a "crosscut" or "pullover" saw and is seldom used for any other role than this. Its suitability for crosscutting lies in the fact that the timber remains stationary whilst being cut as it is the machine head itself which is pulled across the work. The weight and length of the material are, therefore, irrelevant.

As a machine with multi-angle head adjustments, however, its appeal to woodworkers for operations other than simple (or compound angle) crosscutting has been recognised. As a result, the modern, lightweight radial arm saw is marketed as a power source or base for a variety of machining requirements. By swivelling the head through 90 degrees in the horizontal plane, work can be fed along the table and against the fence to achieve a parallel feed for ripping. Attachments and alternaive cutters are also offered for trenching, sanding, routing and jig-sawing. Most of these ancilliary functions understandably fail to match the accuracy or work loading potential of independent, purpose-built machines but they can, nevertheless, be extremely useful in a home workshop where space and cash resources are limited. The basic principles for

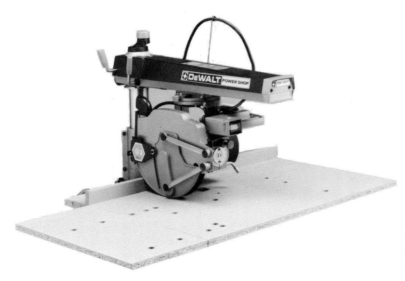

Fig. 97 One of the DeWalt range of radial arm saws. A machine that will prove invaluable in any workshop. (Photo: courtesy Black & Decker, Slough, Bucks.)

Fig. 98 Radial Arm Saw

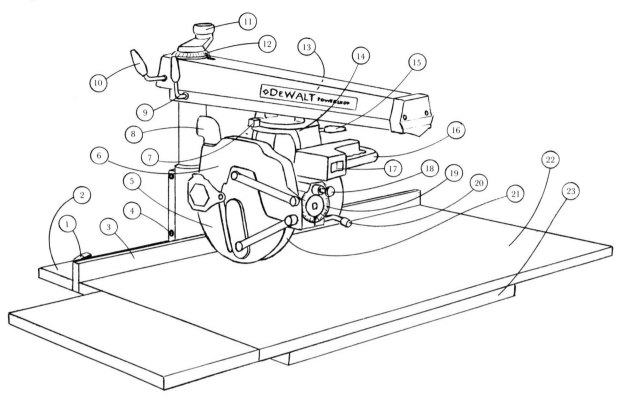

1 Fence and rear table clamp (2)
2 Rear table   3 Removeable fence
4 Friction slide adjusters   5 Gravity guard (outer)
6 "Fixed" guard   7 0°/90°/180°/270° yoke swivel locating stop
8 Waste outlet/extraction point (rubber coupling swivels to direct waste)
9 45°/90°/135° arm swivel locating stop   10 Arm swivel clamp
11 Column rise & fall control   12 Intermediate angle, arm swivel scale
13 Rip lock (locks yoke at any point along radial arm) and rip scales
14 Yoke assembly
15 Yoke swivel clamp   16 Pull handle
17 Secondary ON/OFF switch (T.O.N.V.R. push button starter fitted to frame)
18 0°/45°/90° blade tilt, locating stop
19 Intermediate angle, blade tilt scale
20 Blade tilt clamp   21 Gravity guard (inner)
22 Fixed table   23 Machine frame

the operation of a radial arm saw are the same as for independent machines dealt with in previous chapters. In addition to these, an understanding of the radial arm saw's particular demands when carrying out some operations will be most helpful.

Choice Of Blade

If the saw is to be used primarily for crosscut work then a fine pitch, negative hook blade will give the cleanest possible cut. The backward inclination of each tooth face on this type of blade not only tears the grain to a much lesser extent than a positive hook blade but also reduces the tendency of the motor and saw assembly to be pulled onto the work and jam through sudden overload. (Fig. 99.)

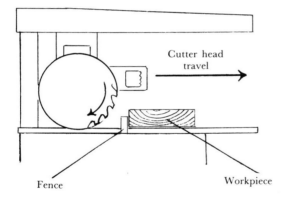

Cutter head travel

Fence

Workpiece

*Fig. 99 The tendency of the travelling machine head is to run forward and climb onto the work due to the fact that blade rotation is assisting rather than resisting the direction of feed. (See the "FIRST GENERAL RULE", Chapter 1). This cannot happen, however, as long as the work is positioned firmly against the fence which prevents it moving **with** the direction of cutter rotation. Even so, to prevent a sudden overload and jam on heavy cuts, it is good practice to pull the machine head along the radial arm with a straight, rather than bent, elbow.*

(A "negative hook" blade reduces this tendency but is more demanding of available power – see Chapter 2).

It is likely in many workshops, however, that the saw will be required for ripsawing operations as well as crosscutting and in this case I would, as with the conventional saw bench, recommend a T.C.T. rip blade as the most useful. This will give acceptable crosscutting performance on any but the most delicate of materials and will permit much faster and deeper rip feeds than would be feasible with a crosscut blade.

Setting Up The Radial Arm Saw

Most radial arm saws are delivered in a partly dismantled state and must be assembled and adjusted for accuracy by the operator. This is no bad thing since it gives him an excellent insight into the method of construction and will enable him to understand the nature of setting problems which will certainly arise from time to time – especially if the saw has been allowed to jam in use. Initial assembly should be carried out in line with the manufacturer's instructions, but when it comes to setting the arm and motor assembly for absolute accuracy some difficulty may be experienced due to the manufacturing tolerances applied and flexibility in the "rigid" components of the machine.

It is important that the three basic or datum settings are accurately made if the saw is to be used for anything other than rough conversion work as the accuracy of all alternative settings depends on these. Firstly, the sawblade will have been mounted directly on the motor shaft and the whole motor/saw assembly will be pulled along the arm to crosscut work laid on the table and against the fence. Obviously if a "square" (i.e. 90 degree) crosscut is required, then the arm must be set to bisect the line of the fence at exactly that angle. (Fig. 100.) Although the actual method of adjustment at the swivel point of the arm is simple enough, the slightest error in setting will be magnified in terms of lateral deviation from the intended line as the saw is pulled along the arm. On lightweight machines it is extremely difficult to make this adjustment with the required degree of accuracy and many machinists build their radial arm saws into a longer, level-set workbench and make a back fence which can itself be adjusted (Fig. 101.)

Fig. 100 The first operation in the setting-up procedure is to adjust the positive 90° stop on the radial arm pivot to ensure that the line of travel of the saw blade is at 90° to the fence. The arm can then be pivoted for angle cutting and returned to this fixed stop as required.

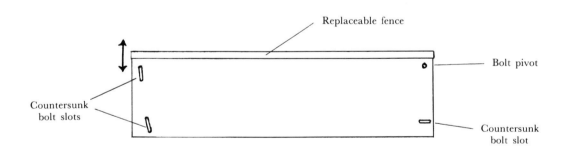

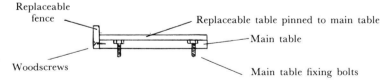

Fig. 101 Fine adjustment of the 90° arm/fence relationship is more easily achieved and maintained by adjusting the fence if the saw is, in any case, to be built into a longer work support bench and necessary modifications can be incorporated at this stage.

Secondly, the line of the saw plate must be adjusted so that it is exactly parallel to the line of the arm. Deviation in this plane will cause pressure from one side of the back of the blade to burn one side of the kerf, or, if the saw is in the rip mode, increase the chances of material rejection. (Fig. 102.)

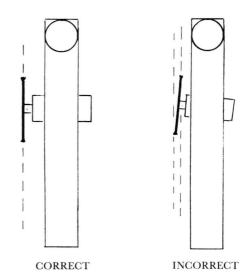

CORRECT   INCORRECT

Fig. 102(a) (right) The saw plate must be parallel to its line of run along the arm so that the rear of the plate follows exactly in the centre of the kerf produced by the cutting action of the forward teeth.

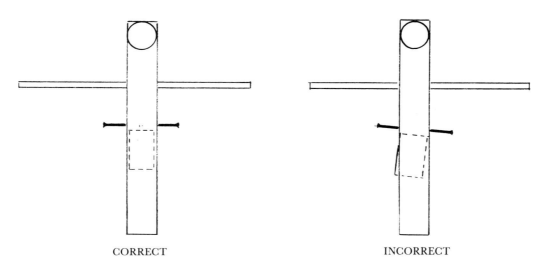

CORRECT   INCORRECT

(b) If the adjustment described in (a) has not been correctly set the saw plate will be out of parallel with the fence when the motor unit is swivelled to either the "in-rip" mode (illustrated) or the out-rip mode.

Finally, the saw plate must be adjusted to a 90 degree vertical relationship with the work support table. It cannot be over-emphasized that the performance of the machine will depend almost entirely on the attention that has been given to these three settings. The operator should feel free to modify or replace the fence and table fixing arrangements where a high degree of accuracy is called for.

A woodworker is better equipped and qualified to make various tables, fences and jigs to improve the accuracy and working convenience of his machine units than almost any other worker. It is a strange fact, however, that so few actually make such improvements, and for some reason prefer to buy items which could easily have been made. The book, *DeWalt Powershop Handbook* (editorial consultant, Gordon Warr) will prove invaluable to owners of radial arm saws of any make in this regard and is full of diagrams and explanations as to how the machine can be adapted and jigged to extend its usefulness.

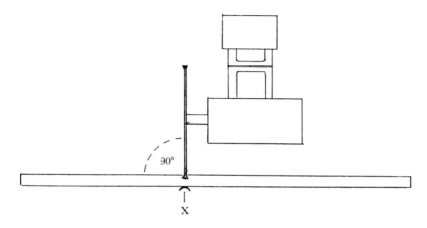

Fig. 103 The saw plate must lastly be set at 90° to the table. (This is the setting most likely to be affected by a sudden jam in crosscutting and should be checked after any such occurrence.)

Where a high degree of accuracy is called for the operator should consider replacing the table with one made from a heavier, distortion-free material as many faults in this setting can be traced to dips and bows in the table surface itself. It may also prove desirable to extend or add to the under-table supporting frame, particularly at line X below the line cut into the table surface by the saw.

Using The Radial Arm Saw

CROSSCUTTING: It can be seen from figure 99 that if the workpiece were fed against the blade, then feed and cutter rotation direction would be the same. This would break the first of the rules described in Chapter One (i.e. **Work must always be fed against the direction of cutter rotation** etc.) with extreme risk of injury to the operator. There are *no* exceptions to this rule in any hand-fed machining operation. It happens that in this case the operation cannot be described as "hand-fed" due to the fact that the saw is pulled across the *stationary* workpiece. The cutting force of the saw blade forces the work onto the table and against the fence so that the work cannot move. The saw blade wants to pull itself onto and over the work but again is prevented from travelling in anything but a predictable, horizontal path due to the controlling rigidity of the arm along which it is being pulled. Consequently, there is no danger to the operator, but even so, on deep crosscuts there is a definite tendency for the saw to pull itself into the work at a rate faster than the saw's ability to cut and clear. The result is a sudden jam, or "crash" as it is sometimes called, when all the momentive energy of the rotating assembly is expended instantaneously, finding the weakest point in its supporting components. In general this will be the point at which adjustments are made and any tolerance or slip in the clamping mechanism will be found and taken up. After such a jam it is quite likely that one of the three critical settings will have been adversely affected necessitating a repeat of the setting-up programme for the machine.

From a point of view of machine setting and maintenance time alone it is important to prevent this occurrence. Industrial radial arm saws will very often be fitted with a hydraulic damper which limits the travel speed of the saw assembly along the arm to a rate at which the saw can work efficiently. Such a unit is available for many lightweight machines and although not essential for timber work, *is vital if the saw is to be used for aluminium frame section cutting*. The effects of a jam when metal cutting are potentially very dangerous indeed and this operation should *never* be undertaken without a new head damper being fitted, as well as the use of an appropriate aluminium cutting blade. As has been pointed out, the only danger in timber crosscutting is to the operator's patience and peace of mind when he finds that precision has been lost after a jam. Having said this, due care must also, of course, be taken to ensure that the left-hand (particularly the thumb) is kept out of the crosscut feed path whatever material is being converted. The easiest way of controlling the tendency to snatch is simply to use a rigid arm when pulling the saw across the workpiece. In other words, the elbow is locked and the pull is made from the shoulder.

After prolonged use the work support fence may have been cut through at a variety of similar angles and no longer be providing adequate backing for offcuts. The danger is that small offcuts in particular, may twist into an excessive aperture under the action of the blade, be picked up and ejected at very high speed. The time taken to make a new fence once the old one has served its useful life will be time well spent.

The gravity guards fitted to many radial saws serve to protect the operator from accidental contact with the sides of the blade when it is parked behind the table fence. Larger, industrial machines will generally have a permanent blade housing behind the fence so that it is completely shrouded when not in use. In any event, care should be taken when cleaning waste from any part of the table, including that behind the fence where, because the saw is not actually operating but running down, vigilance may be relaxed.

Ripping

It is in the saw's ripping mode that mistakes can and have been made with quite spectacular results. It is certainly good policy to read all the instructions and instruction labels that are fitted to the machine or come with it, if you are at all uncertain as to the correct method of use. The principal problem in this regard arises from the fact that the "feed" side of the machine will change in line with the rip mode selected. This is best understood by simple reference to the first rule described in Chapter One. Provided this is appreciated and applied it will be impossible to feed the blade from the wrong side. (Fig. 104) Under no circumstances should this essential requirement be overlooked. Work fed into a saw of this type from the wrong direction will be snatched from the operator, possibly pulling controlling hands with itself and into the blade. As with all machines, work fed onto the back (wrong side) of a rotating

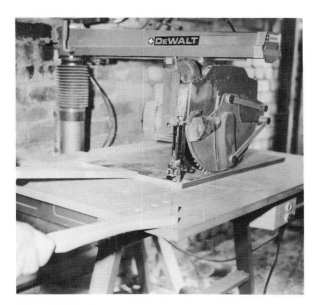

Fig. 104(a) For wider work the saw is swivelled through 180° to the "out-rip" position. Here the work is fed along the fence from left to right.

(b) The "in-rip" mode, where to comply with the first rule (i.e. always feed work **against** the direction of cutter rotation) the workpiece is being fed along the fence from right to left. Note the use of a second push stick to remove the offcut.

cutter will be pulled onto and across it by the cutter action, whereas work fed from the correct side will simply be cut or machined away in direct relation to the feed pressure. As soon as feed pressure is reduced the cut is reduced, and the operator is therefore in complete control.

A further way in which the feed side of the machine can always be established is by consideration of the protection and feed control devices provided by the manufacturers. Reference to Figure 105 will show at a glance that the cutting force exerted on the workpiece is firstly back towards the operator, and secondly, that it is tending to lift the work *off* the table. A work hold-down pressure device to prevent this happening will usually, therefore, be provided at the rip in-feed side of the blade. This either takes the form of an arm which can be lowered and clamped to bear on the workpiece, or the guard may have a leaf

spring attached to its forward edge and the whole guard assembly is swivelled down to provide spring pressure on the workpiece at its in-feed point.

In general there will also be some form of anti-kickback protection but as will be seen from figure 105 this may be at either the in-feed or out-feed side of the blade and should never, therefore, be regarded as an indication of the actual feed side. If a riving knife is fitted to any particular model of radial arm saw then it should always be lowered, clamped and used whenever the saw is in either of the rip modes. (Older models may not have been provided with this protection as they were regarded principally as crosscutting machines and, as has been explained under that section heading, it is the "back" of the blade which is pulled into the work as it lies against the fence. As there is no danger of work "nipping" or closing on the following part of the blade in this

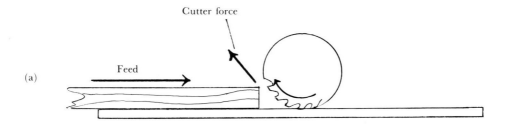

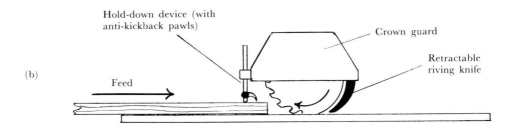

Fig. 105(a) Feed direction is correct but it will be seen that the cutter force is tending to lift the work at the point of cut.

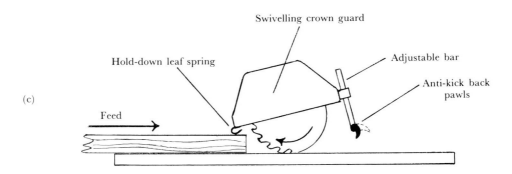

(b) Some means of providing hold-down pressure should be incorporated at the rip in-feed side of the blade. (Anti-kick back fingers may be incorporated at either side according to make and age of the machine.)

The riving knife is lowered for ripping and withdrawn for crosscutting at 90° to the fence.

(c) On some machines the crown guard can be swivelled down to provide hold-down pressure. The adjustable bar with anti-kickback fingers is then sited at the out-feed side of the blade.

Confusion can be avoided by remembering and applying the first rule – "cutter rotation and feed must always be **opposing** *each other at the point of contact."*

operation, a riving knife for crosscutting has not generally been considered essential. It also follows that a riving knife fitted for crosscutting would be on the "wrong" – i.e. rip-in feed – side when the saw was swivelled to one of the rip modes. As radial arm saws became increasingly used for rip sawing, however, many manufacturers, in the interests of improved safety, decided to fit retractable riving knives to their machines – although this is not actually a legal requirement for radial arm saws. Some radial arm saws, therefore, now feature a riving knife that is used in the same way as that fitted to a conventional sawbench at the out-feed side of the blade. In fact, it is the experience of many machinists that the out-feed side of a radial arm saw in the rip position is even more to be respected than that of almost any other machine. Any offcuts or other material allowed to touch the blade at this point will be snatched into extreme compression between the blade and worktable with dramatic and memorable results. The provision of a riving knife is, then, a very welcome addition and one that should be taken full advantage of by the operator.)

Push-sticks, as used for conventional ripping, are also essential for ripping on the radial arm saw. The operator's hand should not pass between the blade and the fence and a push-stick should be used to feed the work through to a line clear of the back of the blade. A push-stick is also very useful for removing offcuts. Many of the general considerations and principles relevant to sawing as discussed in the first two chapters of this book will also be applicable and worth revision.

Mitre Cutting

With the radial arm swung out and clamped at either of the positively located 45 degree positions, it is possible to cut the matching halves of a 90 degree mitred corner joint –

or nearly! The fact is that the smallest error in the original "square" (90 degree to the fence) setting, re-setting or tolerances taken up in clamping will result in an inaccurate joint. This error may not be significant in joinery or carpentry terms, but in the construction of rectangular frames incorporating four related mitres *any* inaccuracy is unacceptable. Being able to set the arm to any angle is nevertheless useful in circumstances where the absolute precision necessary for framing is not called for.

The best system for saw cutting mitre halves to form a *perfect* 90 degree joint is one in which halves of the joint are cut in a fixed 90 degree jig. In this arrangement the saw arm is not moved from its square setting and each frame timber in turn is placed against a 45 degree fence. Provided that the two fences incorporated in the jig have been screwed to the base board at a perfect 90 degrees and the jig is not moved between cuts then the resulting mitre will be absolutely precise. (Fig. 106.) A further obvious advantage is that no time is wasted in re-setting the arm to the opposite hand of the mitre between cuts.

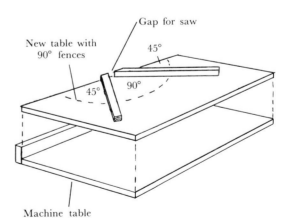

Fig. 106 The new table is made with fences screwed to it in a 90° relationship. When clamped in position against the fence of the existing machine table, perfect 90° mitred corner joints can be cut by using opposite fences for supporting adjacent joint halves without re-setting the radial arm.

Sanding

Sanding is an important part of general woodworking and often the only method by which small components and exposed end-grain sections can be shaped, dimensioned or finished. Almost every power driven spindle or arbor to which some form of sanding device can be fitted will therefore be found useful at some time or other. In the case of the radial arm saw its unique compound angle head setting and large work support area make it doubly attractive for such sanding duties.

A flat disc sanding plate and cylindrical drum sander are available for most models of radial arm saw and, unlike many accessories acquired in the early stages of setting up a machine and subsequently never used, will come to be highly valued.

Even though sanders have no rotating metal teeth to concern the user they can nevertheless remove a great deal of material from objects in contact with them *very* quickly indeed. The operator should not, therefore, approach or use them with a casual attitude. As with cutting tools of any type, maximum control of the workpiece will be achieved when it is fed *against* the direction of cutter rotation. Observance of this principle becomes essential, even with sanders, in any captive machining operation such as "back fencing" (see Chapter Four) with a drum sander, and where work or fingers could be pulled into compression between drum and fence.

Trenching

A variable width saw or cutter can be used in place of the standard saw blade to machine rebates, groves or trenches of considerable width and depth in a single pass. The two tools most commonly used for this operation are the "Wobble Saw" and the "Dado Head". The wobble saw is a saw blade mounted on specially machined collars which can be set to produce varying amounts of lateral throw in the blade. The sides of a groove produced with a wobble saw will be parallel but the bottom of the groove will show a concave section matching the radius of the saw plate and may limit its usefulness on wide grooves or rebates where this effect will be more noticeable.

The dado head produces grooves with parallel sides and a square bottom. It may be of the type which consists of two flat saw plates packed out to the desired width with chipping irons mounted on the shaft between them or, the more sophisticated overlap grooving blocks or discs spaced with shims as shown in Figure 107.

No particular precautions other than those applicable to any rotating machine cutterhead need be taken, but it should be noted that a trenching head is often removing a considerable amount of material on each revolution and the forces at work will be proportionate. For example, in using a dado head on a radial arm saw in its crosscutting mode, say, for trenching cabinet sides to accept shelves, there will be an increased tendency for the cutter to pull itself into the work and jam. This should be checked in the same way as it is checked for heavy crosscutting: that is, with a locked elbow and slow, straight arm pull from the shoulder.

Moulding

The performance of most radial arm saws set up for moulding operations may, understandably, be a disappointment if the operator expects results comparable to those he is used to achieving with the vertical spindle moulder. It may, however, be the only method of moulding available to him and as such can be very useful if due allowance is made for the lower rotational speed of the cutter-block and consequently reduced momentive energy. In practice this will mean that much lower feed speeds have to be used than with a conventional spindle moulder to avoid cutter pitch marks and to avoid the problem of even further reducing the cutter's peripheral speed and running into the danger area where it becomes impossible for the knives to cut at all. When this point is reached a kickback will occur. Provided that the cutter-block is allowed to rotate at something approaching its free running speed there is no danger of this happening. As with all machines, explore its potential progressively, starting with large workpieces and light cut settings until you have developed a "feel" for the operation. The general principles of moulding explained in Chapter Four are equally applicable to the radial arm saw when set for this purpose and should be understood.

An important point that should be noted arises from the instructions given by some manufacturers and suppliers. For reasons best known to themselves and beyond the ken of any woodmachinist, they offer a moulding block and *single* cutters for use with the radial arm saw. Their suggestion is that a so-called "balancing" cutter be fitted opposite the profile cutter instead of a matching profile cutter. It is obvious that the only cutter which can actually balance another in this particular tool is another identical cutter. *My advice to any operator is most certainly not to use any rotating cutter assembly which is unbalanced.* The vibration set up in a lightweight machine running in this state may well be transmitted through the table and fences to the body of the workpiece, spoiling proper control contact and resulting in an accident. In addition, the strain placed on the machine components themselves is dangerous and unnecessary.

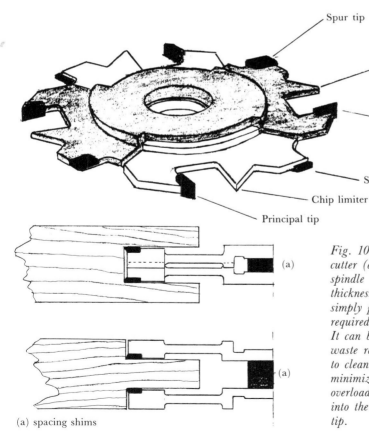

Spur tip (upper)

Chip limiter

Principal tip

Spur tip (lower)

Chip limiter

Principal tip

(a) spacing shims

(a)

(a)

Fig. 107 *This pattern of expanding grooving cutter (dado) is available for both saws and spindle moulders in a variety of diameters and thicknesses. The two segments of the tool are simply packed apart to vary the overlap as required. (For clarity the top segment is shaded.) It can be seen that in addition to the principal waste removing tips, "spur" tips are incorporated to clean the walls of the groove. Also, to minimize any possibility of kick-back when overloading, chip thickness limiters are moulded into the tool body in front of each main cutting tip.*

CHAPTER SEVEN

The Woodturning Lathe

Many excellent books on this subject are available explaining how different turners solve the problems of controlling hand held tools through fast moving wood. This is an area of woodworking in which the student may find himself becoming confused at the seemingly contradictory advice often given by different authors. My advice in this regard is simply to try alternative methods of achieving the same results and, if the results are acceptable, use the method. It is, after all, an acquired, manual skill and it should not be expected or necessary to describe variations of technique as "right" or "wrong", simply because an individual pronounces them so. Provided that the basic and essential requirements for safety are observed, then it can be said that there are probably as many ways of carrying on productive and enjoyable woodturning as there are woodturners. Each turner will develop variations of technique which *he* finds useful. The following section, therefore, lays out the simple guidelines within which this most fascinating and potentially rewarding craft can be practised.

Fig. 108 The performance of any bench lathe can be improved significantly by mounting it on a heavyweight stand. A trough has been formed between the top rails of this bench and filled with concrete. (The Arundel lathe shown features a sliding headstock so that large diameters can be turned over the right hand end of the lathe bed.) (Photo: courtesy Treebridge Ltd., Newark, Notts.)

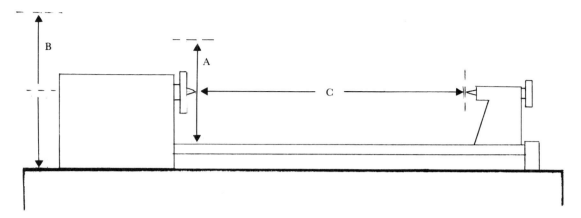

Fig. 109 A: Maximum diameter that can be turned over the lathe bed, or
"Swing over bed".

B: Maximum diameter that can be turned by any other means
(i.e. "outboard" turning, swivelling headstock or sliding
headstock) – simply termed "Maximum swing".

C: Maximum length that can be turned between centres
referred to as 835mm/33" centres, 900mm/36" centres etc.

The Lathe

Remembering that this machine of all woodworking machines is the one that will have to absorb very considerable out-of-balance rotating forces, its own weight and consequent inertia will be its most valuable asset. All other things being equal, a heavy lathe will be one which is more enjoyable to use and actually speeds production due to the absence of vibration and the feasibility of taking fine and accurate finishing cuts. Anything that can be done to increase the weight and strength of a lightweight machine will therefore be well worth-while. The simplest method of achieving this is usually to build extra weight into the stand or base of the machine with panelling and sandbag or concrete block ballast.

Lathes are specified by "swing", which refers to the maximum diameter of work which can be mounted (Fig. 109) and by "centres", which is the term used to describe the maximum distance between the head and tailstock centres and therefore the maximum theoretical length of work which can be accommodated. It should be understood that the advertised *theoretical* capacity of any particular lathe may not be a realistic safe *working* capacity, and in fact *no* hand turning lathe I have ever seen is actually capable of turning a workpiece that measures maximum swing and distance between centres combined.

For general turning requirements a lathe offering a swing of around 350 or 375 mm (14"–15") is adequate and a disc or bowl blank of 350 mm × 100 mm (14" × 4") is approaching the real capacity limits of the vast majority of lathes offered for small professional or home workshops. Similarly, a 900 mm × 100 mm (36" × 4") workpiece mounted between centres can be quite large enough to prompt a thoughtful chewing of the lower lip as the lathe is about to be switched on, and an extended bed to increase centre capacity may have little practical value if the lathe is lightweight or insubstantial. In the case of hand turning in particular (as against industrial automatic

(a)

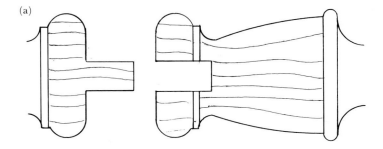

Fig. 110(a) Work which is too long for the lathe or too thin to be turned without excessive whip can be broken down before turning and jointed on loose or turned dowels. The joint should be made where two features come together in a 'V'.

(b)

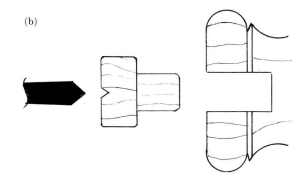

(b) Joint holes should be pre-drilled so that the tailstock centre can be centred on the hole itself (plugged as illustrated if necessary) when mounting the workpiece. The turning and joint will then be perfectly concentric.

turning), most turners find it best to break down long workpieces into shorter lengths and dowel joint them after turning. If the holes necessary for this type of joint are drilled before the turning is done then the joint can be contrived so that it is completely undetectable. (Fig. 110.)

Lathe Speeds

A handturning lathe must have a range of headstock spindle speeds suited to its workholding capacities so that large and heavy workpieces can be turned safely. Different turners will often choose to turn similarly dimensioned workpieces at different speeds and there is no *absolute* rule in this regard other than that the larger the diameter of the work or the greater its length and weight, the slower the initial turning speed should be. In other words, until experience has been gained, always start the

lathe at a low speed to check that no excessive vibration is likely to occur. Keep the lathe at this speed at least until the work has been trued sufficiently to reduce vibration to acceptable levels.

As a rough guide, faceplate work of around 200 mm (8″) or more in diameter should be started at the lowest lathe speed (usually around 400–600 rpm) and, after truing, shaped at a slightly higher speed. Spindle work of over 100 mm (4″) in thickness should also be checked for possible run-out at one of the lower lathe speeds, and particularly so as the length of the workpiece increases. Then, in relation to its length and weight the piece can be turned at a speed of perhaps 1000–1500 rpm. Smaller diameter spindles or very short ones can safely be turned at 2000 rpm or even faster in the case of balanced work. Every turner will eventually select speeds in the light of his own experience. The important and guiding factor will be that the speed is such that excessive vibration and consequent stress on workpiece holding devices is avoided.

The actual speeds incorporated in lathes made especially for the English speaking market range from approximately 500 rpm to a top speed of 2000–2500 rpm with one or two intermediate speeds. These spindle speeds should not be regarded as critical from the point of view of work finish but, as stated, important from a safety standpoint. Obviously, a 300 mm (12″) disc turning at 600 rpm incorporates within itself every diameter from zero to 300 mm (12″) and every part of the disc can be successfully cut and faced at this speed. The choice of the 600 rpm spindle speed would be to avoid too high a peripheral speed. It follows that a smaller disc of say 75 mm (3″) diameter could also be turned at 600 rpm. The point of using a higher speed would simply be to speed the workrate by avoiding "screw-threading" or spiral ridging left by a traversing tool and more waste material can therefore be removed in an equivalent time without leaving visible tool marks. Some turners also prefer to sand and polish work at a slightly higher speed than that used for shaping.

Work Mounting

It is, of course, essential that work mounted in the lathe is secure. The traditional methods for mounting spindles, bowls, platters and hollow-ware are shown in Figure 111 and should be available for every lathe. More recently a range of expanding and gripping collet chucks have been introduced to supplement the faceplate and provide a most convenient means of mounting bowls, etc., without the need for holding screws. Some of the these chucks can also be adapted for spigot and screw chuck duties. These are particularly useful for repetition work where a secure and subsequently invisible single-point mounting is called for. (Fig. 112.)

(a)

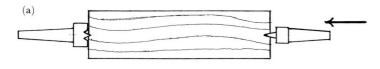

Fig. 111(a) CENTRES: work is held and compressed against the pronged drive centre by pressure from the tailstock centre. The tailstock centre may be 'dead' (does not revolve), or 'live' (turns with the work).

(b)

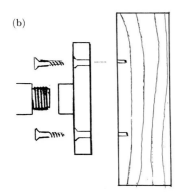

(b) FACEPLATE: work is held by woodscrews inserted through the back of the plate. Bowl turning requires successive mountings – first to turn the outside and foot of the bowl, secondly, reversing the work to finish the inside. In this second stage the work can either be screwed to the faceplate, glued to a piece of scrap and separated after turning, or a recess the diameter of the foot be scraped in a piece of scrap screwed to the plate, and the foot of the bowl simply held in it by friction.
*(**Note**: Corners must be removed so that the work is roughly disc shaped on any workpiece mounted with the grain running predominantly **across**, rather than along, the bed)*

(c)

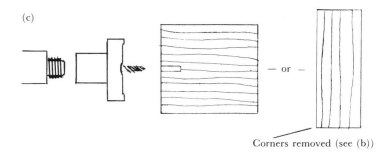

– or –

Corners removed (see (b))

(c) *CENTRE SCREW CHUCK: Work is held by being screwed directly onto a woodscrew locked in and protruding from the chuck body.*

Best grip is obtained if a pilot hole is drilled for the centre screw. Grip is further improved by provision of a raised lip around the edge of the chuck face to aid positive seating. (A slightly concave faced wooden packing disc can be made to fill this role if necessary.)

(d)

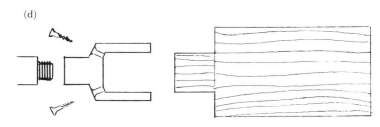

(d) *CUP CHUCK: Useful where long-grain work has to be mounted with an 'open' end (no support from tailstock) and length/weight of work is such that a screw chuck provides insufficient grip.*

A spigot equal to the cup diameter is turned by first mounting the work between centres.

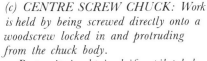

Fig. 112(a) The "MULTISTAR DUPLEX CHUCK" incorporates a mechanism which permits the collets to be used in a contracting or expanding mode. Collets are available in a wide range of diameters. Many other work holding and driving accessories can be directly loaded into the chuck mouth.

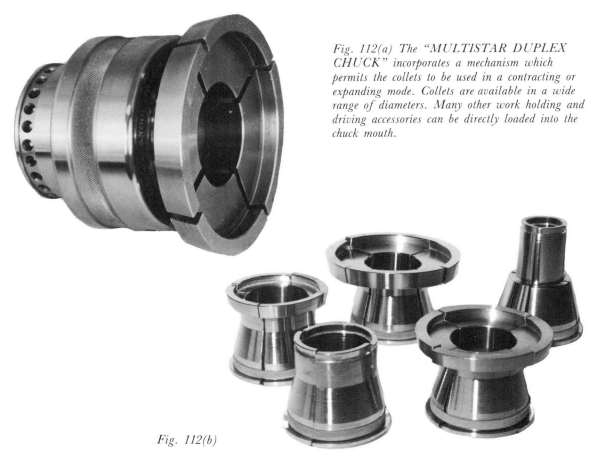

Fig. 112(b)

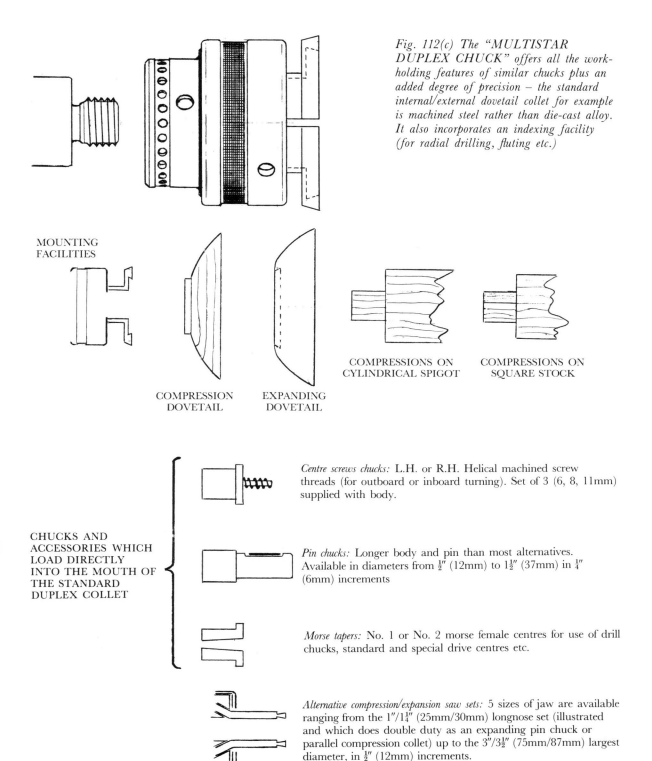

Fig. 112(c) The "MULTISTAR DUPLEX CHUCK" offers all the work-holding features of similar chucks plus an added degree of precision – the standard internal/external dovetail collet for example is machined steel rather than die-cast alloy. It also incorporates an indexing facility (for radial drilling, fluting etc.)

MOUNTING FACILITIES

COMPRESSION DOVETAIL

EXPANDING DOVETAIL

COMPRESSIONS ON CYLINDRICAL SPIGOT

COMPRESSIONS ON SQUARE STOCK

CHUCKS AND ACCESSORIES WHICH LOAD DIRECTLY INTO THE MOUTH OF THE STANDARD DUPLEX COLLET

Centre screws chucks: L.H. or R.H. Helical machined screw threads (for outboard or inboard turning). Set of 3 (6, 8, 11mm) supplied with body.

Pin chucks: Longer body and pin than most alternatives. Available in diameters from $\frac{1}{2}''$ (12mm) to $1\frac{1}{2}''$ (37mm) in $\frac{1}{4}''$ (6mm) increments

Morse tapers: No. 1 or No. 2 morse female centres for use of drill chucks, standard and special drive centres etc.

Alternative compression/expansion saw sets: 5 sizes of jaw are available ranging from the $1''/1\frac{1}{4}''$ (25mm/30mm) longnose set (illustrated and which does double duty as an expanding pin chuck or parallel compression collet) up to the $3''/3\frac{1}{2}''$ (75mm/87mm) largest diameter, in $\frac{1}{2}''$ (12mm) increments.

101

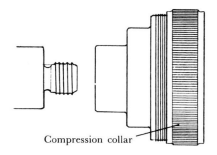

Compression collar

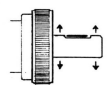

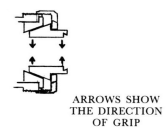

ARROWS SHOW
THE DIRECTION
OF GRIP

Fig. 112(d) The "PRECISION COMBINATION CHUCK" is an excellent example of several multi-chuck systems now available for holding virtually any type of work in the lathe. The principal work holding devices shown below are simply interchanged in the chuck mouth to provide the required grip.

Expanding dovetail collets: Screwing the compression collar back pulls the four-piece dovetail collet onto a coned centre boss in the chuck body which in turn forces the collet to expand. The workpiece is prepared by scraping a dovetail recess of the appropriate diameter into its base.

Split rings: For turning substantial long-grain workpieces without support from the tailstock 3 piece split ring sets can be used in the mouth of the chuck. Work is first prepared between centres with a stepped spigot and groove for the split ring to sit in. Screwing the compression collar back then locks the prepared end inside the chuck against the reversed centre boss.

Pin chucks: Various diameters of pin are available for gripping hollow spindles (pepermills etc.) without the risk of splitting associated with expanding chucks. A loose pin roller sits on a flat in the cylindrical chuck body and rolls to lock the work on the chuck as soon as the work begins to resist the drive rotation. Unlocking (with the work stationary) is achieved by twisting the work **with** the direction of normal rotation, causing the roller pin to move back to its free centre.

Centre screw chuck: The operational principle and uses of this attachment are exactly as explained in Fig. 112c. This chuck does however provide a very much improved grip as the centre screw is a properly machined, parallel screw rather than the conventional woodscrew otherwise used. Work is prepared by drilling a pilot hole.

Compression collets: As the compression collar is screwed back onto the chuck body the collet is forced into a female cone which causes a parallel contraction of the collet tube segments. Extremely useful for repetition turning of dowel stock and involving less preparation than any alternative system of single end fixing where a really strong grip is required. The grip movement of 6mm ($\frac{1}{4}''$) also allows for considerable variation of stock dowel diameter.

Tools and Tool Sharpening

To cut efficiently tools must be sharp and be of a steel compound which is sufficiently hard to keep a good cutting edge for a reasonable length of time in service. In the case of carbon steel compounds of which good quality traditional edge tools are made, extreme hardness induced by heating and quenching results in extreme brittleness. This of course can be dangerous if the steel is subjected to a bending load as may sometimes happen in woodturning and when as a result the tool may shatter. To avoid this problem tools are tempered by re-heating to a lower temperature. This has the effect of inducing resilience but also adversely affects edge-holding characteristics.

Manufacturing tools to combine the essentials of hardness and resilience is an exacting and highly skilled process and it is unwise from every point of view to economise on the tools themselves. In my opinion it is also unwise to adapt any piece of steel for use as a woodturning tool simply because it holds a good edge, although I know of many woodturners (who have my respect as craftsmen) who do use tempered files as scraping tools. Even so, my advice is still the same: use tools of a reputable make and which are sold specifically for the purpose for which you intend to use them.

As an alternative to carbon steel tools there are now available HSS (High Speed Steel) tools for turning, and although I have little personal experience of them I am assured by many of my woodturning friends that they represent a significant development in this field. Their principal advantage lies in the fact that they are of such extreme hardness (and strength under bending stress) that they require much less frequent sharpening. My reluctance to switch from the tools with which I earned a living for many years lies simply in the fact that once mastery of the dry grinding wheel has been gained the average carbon steel tool can be re-ground in a matter of seconds, whereas high speed steel takes much longer.

Tool sharpening in general is probably the area of activity (or inactivity), to which the greatest number of problems in tool control on the lathe can be traced. Perseverance in this field will be amply repaid and the absolute necessity for recognition of the relationship between predictable results in tool application and sharp tools cannot be over-emphasized. Controversy about tool sharpening continues to preoccupy theorists in the columns of the woodworking magazines and I must confess to having at times become one of them. Having previously stated in this chapter that there are as many ways to turn wood as there are woodturners, basic common-sense guidelines accepted, I do feel irritated when the experience of professional men (earning-a-living, that is) is dismissed as irrelevant by some who should recognize that others can produce the same results as they by different methods. I am quite prepared in *this* context to acknowledge these rights, as patently, there are many superb woodturners who sharpen their tools by methods I do not. The point that *must* be agreed is that all cutting tools must be sharp. With due deference to others then, I would say that *I* have found direct, dry grinding to be the most practical way of inducing a good working edge on woodturning tools. The slight, almost microscopic, irregularities that result act much as the teeth of a saw blade in reducing heat concentration through friction at the cutting edge of the tool. It takes literally a few seconds to freshen such an edge on the grinding wheel and time in woodturning is best spent at woodturning rather than pursuit of perfection in honing an edge that will inevitably be lost within the first few hundred feet of work contact – perhaps one or two minutes.

Neither, again with due deference to purists, are bevel angles the infallible answer to tool control. Within reason, the "sharpness" angles of woodturning tools are a matter of personal preference – fairly acute angles being generally preferred for softwoods and more obtuse (blunter or steeper) angles giving more support to the cutting edge when working denser timbers. (Fig. 113.)

Experience in, and familiarity with, tool sharpening is a key factor in the genuinely attainable satisfaction of woodturning. Perseverance in this direction is much more to the point than the acquisition of chucks and tools in addition to basic requirements in the early stages of the craft.

Fig. 113 The sharpness angle of turning tools is not of critical importance. An acute angle with consequently long bevel (a) is generally preferred for softwoods whereas a "blunter" angle (not cutting edge!) with shorter bevel gives more support to the cutting edge when working hardwoods. In both cases the tool must be angled to maintain bevel/work contact.

Scrapers, (c) which are used in a trailing attitude at centre height, are ground almost square to give maximum strength to the working edge.

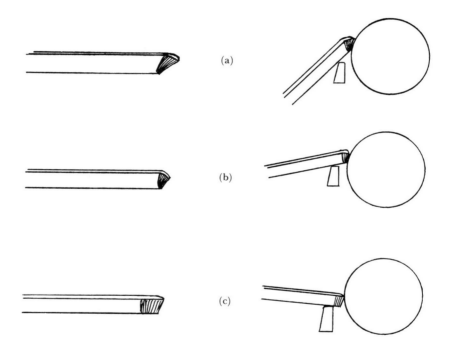

(a)

(b)

(c)

Attention to the grinding wheel itself is important if good results are to be obtained without overheating the tool edges. An "open" face must be maintained so that the sharp, abrasive edges of the grit particles can cut away unwanted metal. I have found that most grinding wheels fitted to double-ended bench grinders as standard are suitable for sharpening and re-shaping hand turning tools provided they are properly "dressed". "Dressing" is the process of removing the glazed surface layer which builds progressively on the working face of a grinding wheel in use. A rotary type dressing tool is best for this maintenance procedure as it removes the blunted surface particles of the wheel by a crushing action, thereby leaving the sharp cutting edges of underlying abrasive particles exposed. A "Devil Stone" on the other hand removes abraded particles by a superior abrasive action and therefore tends to reduce the cool cutting potential of the freshly exposed particles. A freshly dressed wheel may require a little "running in" before its performance can be guaranteed. I have found that sharpening a square-ended scraper with slightly more pressure than would normally be used is effective in removing minor surface irregularities and dust which are left after dressing. Also, irrespective of the transparent plastic eye shield which must be fitted to all bench grinders, personal eye protection should be worn.

Tool Control

Both from a general safety standpoint and predictable cutting performance, it is important that a few simple procedures are observed. A little thought about the nature of the forces likely to be encountered when applying any selected tool to rotating timber makes the need for such procedural concepts apparent. Figure 114 shows the action of a hand-held gouge cutting away a predictable thickness of timber from a stationary workpiece. The bevel of the tool is in direct contact with the work surface and it is this which controls the thickness of shaving removed. The bevel is bearing on the freshly revealed surface exposed by the cutting edge. If the angle of tool presentation is altered, say by lifting the tool handle, then only the cutting edge itself will bear on the work surface and, under pressure from the carver's hand, will enter the workpiece until it again finds support from the bevel. Conversely, if the handle of the tool is lowered, then the cutting edge will be lifted away from the timber by the leverage of the bevel heel and no amount of pressure from the carver's hand will induce the cutting edge to enter the work. The woodcarver will therefore start a fine shaving cut with the tool held at a "safe" angle (that is, with only the heel of the bevel in direct work contact) and then progressively raise the tool handle until he finds the angle at which the cutting edge barely begins to bite. Provided this angle of tool presentation is maintained then a controlled and even thickness of timber will be removed on each forward stroke of the tool.

In woodturning practice the same basic

Fig. 114

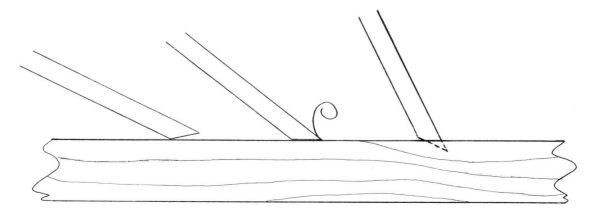

principle applies. The only difference is that the feed roles of tool and timber are now reversed with the tool being held stationary and the timber being fed under it at high speed. A grasp of this basic principle will be an enormous help in post-mortem analysis of mistakes and in future development of clean-cutting technique. A useful excercise to the end of acquiring the essential "feel" for bevel/work contact is as follows:

1. Mount a length of 50 mm (2") square timber between centres so that the grain runs parallel to the bed. For convenience in this instance it will be helpful if the workpiece is about 50 mm (2") shorter overall than the length of the toolrest so that this component will not have to be repositioned and concentration can be directed uninterruptedly towards the work in hand.

2. Check that the lathe is set to run at a suitable speed in relation to the diameter being turned. (This is a good habit to get into even if you *know* that the workpiece diameter is such that it can be turned safely at the maximum speed setting of your lathe. An excessively heavy or out-of-balance workpiece accelerated from rest to 2500 or 3000 rpm may well decide to leave its mountings with painful or, at best, memorable consequences.)

3. Position the toolrest as closely as possible to the workpiece and check work clearance by hand through its full 360 degree rotation.

4. Re-check that all work mounting clamps, fixings and tool-post/cross-slide locking devices are secure. (Although the woodturning lathe is one of the safest of all machines due to the fact that it has no rotating cutter assemblies, accidents can nevertheless happen and it is good practice to follow a habitual system of routine checks *before* switching on, irrespective of assumption.

5. Switch on. (This is an exciting moment if you have never previously attempted woodturning and a momentary suspension of normal breathing processes is acceptable provided it does not lead to unconsciousness.)

6. Place a spindle gouge or roughing gouge on the *toolrest*. (This may seem superfluous to the dictates of common sense, but it is surprising how often students at this stage of their turning career forget to place the tool firmly on the toolrest *before* letting it touch the rotating timber. As my good friend Gordon Stokes once remarked, "If you don't put the tool on the rest, the wood soon will!") Additionally, the tool must be presented to the work at a "safe" angle as shown in figure 115 so that as it is advanced over the toolrest into contact with the work it is the *heel* of the bevel which makes initial contact rather than the cutting edge. This will be felt as a knocking on the bevel. No matter how much additional forward pressure is applied through the handle of the tool at this point, no chip or shaving can be removed until the *angle* of tool presentation is altered.

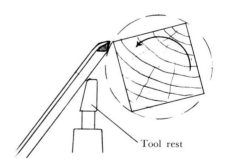

Tool rest

Fig. 115 *For safety the gouge is angled so that initially only the heel of the bevel makes work contact. As the handle is raised an angle will be reached where the cutting edge begins to enter the rotational arc of the workpiece and a chip will be removed from each corner.*

Note: *Cross-grain mounted work must be sawn to a rough disc before turning. (See also Fig. 111)*

This forward pressure of tool bevel against work is the turner's first experience of positive tool control. It should be "felt" and understood as the key to future success in hand turning.

Raising the handle of the gouge slowly whilst maintaining slight forward pressure so that the cutting edge is brought to bear will remove a small chip. The gouge should then be rolled and inclined *slightly* in the intended direction of traverse and, maintaining bevel contact pressure, run along the work and off. Return the gouge to the centre of the rest and repeat the procedure in the opposite direction.

Most turning problems are traceable to non-observance of, or unfamiliarity with, this essential principle of tool control.

The second principle of tool control is simply to work from large to small diameters, or "downhill" on work mounted between centres. It is certainly not impossible to run a tool "uphill" on shallow gradients but it does become increasingly difficult to maintain control as the hill steepens. For a novice turner, any attempt to work uphill will almost certainly result in a dig-in. The reasons for this have been explored in depth in various writings (including my own in *Woodworker* and *Practical Woodworking* magazines) but for the purposes of this section a simple statement of the fact is all that is really necessary.

Lastly, use the portion of the cutting edge which corresponds to the portion of the tool shaft supported on the toolrest. This may sound complicated, but reference to figure 116 will make the principle clearer. It can be seen that when cuts are made in this way there is no tendency for the tool to twist due to the leverage factor exerted when an unsupported part of the cutting edge is used.

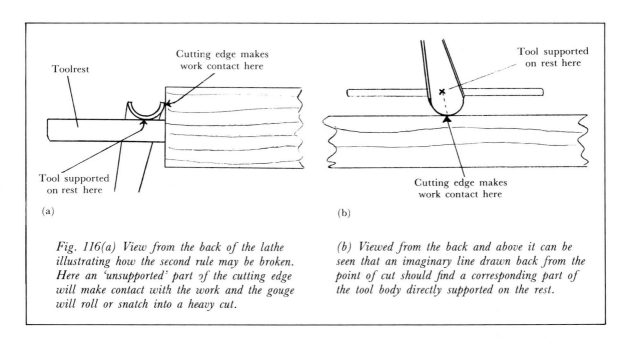

(a)

(b)

Fig. 116(a) View from the back of the lathe illustrating how the second rule may be broken. Here an 'unsupported' part of the cutting edge will make contact with the work and the gouge will roll or snatch into a heavy cut.

(b) Viewed from the back and above it can be seen that an imaginary line drawn back from the point of cut should find a corresponding part of the tool body directly supported on the rest.

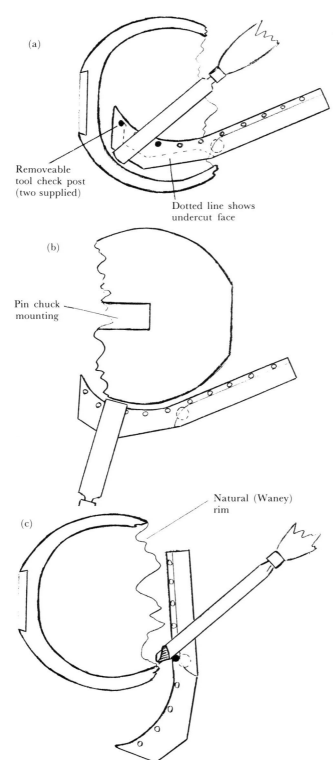

(a)

Removeable
tool check post
(two supplied)

Dotted line shows
undercut face

(b)

Pin chuck
mounting

Natural (Waney)
rim

(c)

Fig. 117

The "Multi-Rest" is a recent introduction to the range of accessories available to woodturners and overcomes many of the problems experienced in bowl turning with conventional toolrests.

Fig. 117(a) Conventional (straight) toolrests are frequently unable to provide support as close to remote faces as is ideal. Curved rests partially overcome this problem but – particularly when used for flat bladed scraping tools – allow the tool to rock laterally as it is raised from the horizontal plane to effect the necessary trailing (nose-down) attitude.

The "Multi-Rest" provides stable and predictable support for tools in virtually any position for bowl hollowing work by breaking the line of its "convex" edge into a series of straight edges.

(b) External scraping without over-frequent repositioning of the rest is catered for by using the concave edge. Here the tool is always supported across its width once the handle has been slightly elevated and again, perfect control is assured.

(Tool chatter is further dampened by virtue of the fact that the Multi-Rest is a solid iron casting weighing approximately eight pounds – compared with an average one to two pounds for most standard rests)

(c) The straight section of the rest is bevelled on the turner's side for use with conventional gouges and so that the support edge is thrown forward as far as possible. The tool check post can be removed and positioned in any of the pre-drilled holes to prevent lateral tear-out of the gouge as rim incising cuts are made. This is especially helpful when working natural rimmed bowls where the gouge initially finds little support for its bevel.

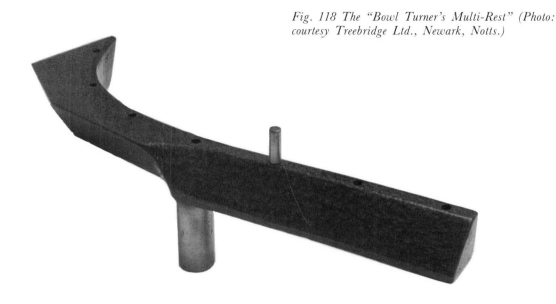

Fig. 118 The "Bowl Turner's Multi-Rest" (Photo: courtesy Treebridge Ltd., Newark, Notts.)

Developing Technique

Rather like learning to ride a bicycle where perhaps years of studying bike riding theory will be of little value in actually riding the machine, so too, it is possible to become over-involved in the theoretical aspects of woodturning and never develop the practical familarity with clean cutting techniques so essential to enjoyment of the craft. True, a knowledge of basic rules will help you to analyse your mistakes and help you avoid the more painful ones but ultimately it is practice, practice and more practice which will enable you reveal the shape you see hidden in a piece of timber. Start your turning as suggested, by simply roughing down a cylinder from the square. This will help in overcoming any initial nervousness and assist in the business of sensing what is happening at the tool's tip. Then, following the instructions gleaned from the pages of any well written book on turning, practice simple cuts with the different categories of tool.

Once you have had this experience, which need be no more than a brief familiarization, I would suggest a self-teaching plan that may at first glance seem unappealing but one which I promise is the most remarkably effective way of learning to turn ever!

Cut fifty egg cup blanks, say 50 mm (2″) × 50 mm (2″) × 70 mm (2¾″) in length. Mount the first on a suitable screwchuck and have a go at it. Incorporated in such a simple project will be most of the shapes, or basic cuts necessary to make those shapes, which are ever likely to be needed to produce almost any item on the lathe. Don't become despondent when you make a mistake. If the piece is still on the lathe, finish it and immediately mount a second piece. You now have the opportunity to try the same cut again. You may or may not make the same mistake – whatever, by the time you have made the same mistake a dozen or so times in succession you will be well aware of the problem itself and well on the way to beginning an analysis of your technique so that you can overcome or at least side-step the difficulty. Put aside the first egg cup you make in this batch of fifty and note exactly how long it took to produce. Carry on through the day until you have completed the full fifty. Now compare the first and the last egg cups and I guarantee that you will be delighted with your progress, both in regard to the time taken to make them and in the work finish, not to mention your own confidence.

This may seem like an uninviting prospect, the mere word "repetition" being somehow alien to the concept of craft, but it need not be so. Particularly in the early stages of learning, the greatest and most satisfying leaps in turning ability can be made in just this way. In fact, I would go as far as to say that this is really the *only* way to develop real fluency of turning technique. Additionally, the fact that you are using small workpieces to practise these skills means that you will be uninhibited by cost or adrenalin surges when things go wrong. Alternatively, you can start and continue your turning career by making a great variety of interesting "one-off" projects, or even half a dozen of these, and those without ever making significant progress in *real* turning technique. True, in time, your work may be indistinguishable from that of a master turner. The difference of course will be that he can produce the same article in a fraction of the time and will enjoy the actual process of turning as it happens rather than simply working in anticipation of the finished piece. Turners who persist in this approach, that is, ones and twos, do develop a sort of survival cunning by using some cutting tools as scrapers and by avoiding the use of some tools altogether. *After* you have turned your first "fifty-off" and *before* you abandon the use of the skew chisel for end-grain facing and invent other "safe" methods of changing the shape of the workpiece, go on a woodturning course.

Now you will have experienced most of the problems likely to occur in handturning and will really get the full benefit of personal and qualified instruction. Attending such a course before you have had any *controlled* experience of the lathe is, to my mind, to lose more than half its potential benefit. Under these circumstances at least 50 percent of the course time will be taken up with the instructor explaining the nature of the problems themselves. You therefore have to learn problems and solutions. If you have experienced the problems you can immediately relate to their solution.

Finally, as with all machinery, learn to use it progressively. Think about everything you do before you do it and follow the advice of turners who have experience in teaching this most rewarding of woodworking crafts.

CHAPTER EIGHT

Other Independent Machines

Apart from the "classic" workshop machines dealt with in preceding sections, there are some other independent (or single-purpose) units which may be useful in busy shops or where workshop output is specialized. In the main the operation of these requires little or no additional grasp of machining principle other than that applicable to the operation of any wood cutting or shaping machine.

Mortisers:

Slot Mortisers: This type of mortiser is the most useful for very fast production of comparatively shallow mortises such as those required in the construction of cabinet frames, tables, chairs and so on. The nature of the cutting tool means that the slot produced will have parallel sides and a flat bottom but radiused ends. These can be "squared" with a hand chisel if required or tenons rounded to match. It will be found when working with shouldered tenons that cutting the parallel faces of the tongue *slightly* longer than the parallel sides of the mortise (if this has been left with radiused ends) ensures positive location and of course saves the rounding or squaring time. Very little strength is lost by this method but obviously any loss of strength may be undesirable if the joint is required to bear heavy loads.

Safety in the operation of slot mortisers is very much a matter of taking the obvious precautions such as keeping loose clothing, neck ties and fingers away from the rotating bit and chuck. Always ensure that the chuck key has been removed before switching on. (Flying chuck keys are the most common cause of injury on machines of this type. Checking that any tool is free to rotate through its full cycle is one of the rules discussed in Chapter One and provided this has been done an accident of the nature described cannot occur.) Also, as always, the chuck and cutter must be enclosed to the greatest extent that is practicable and in this case a plastic guard over the top of the cutter may meet this requirement.

If, as shown in figure 121, your slot mortiser is attached to the side of a planer/thicknesser machine, then the mortising bit will be held in a chuck which is an extension of the machine cutter-block. This means that the cutter-block will be running when the mortiser is in use and MUST BE FULLY COVERED BY CLAMPED GUARDS ON BOTH SIDES OF THE PLANER FENCE. Your attention in every machining operation will be concentrated on the work in hand and it must never be possible to touch any part of the machine, other than that necessarily exposed to carry out the work intended, and sustain injury. Slot mortising bits have a bottom, or plunge cutting action so that they can drill into the work, and a side

Fig. 119 (left) Hollow chisel mortiser. (Photo: courtesy Multico Ltd., Redhill, Surrey.)

Fig. 120 (bottom left) The hollow chisel mortiser offers the advantage of being able to cut rectangular, flat bottomed mortises. The long lever controls the plunge, the large handwheel the table traverse and the small handwheel below it the back or fore positioning of the table. (Photo: courtesy J. Fox & Sons, Cardiff.)

Fig. 121 (below) A slot mortiser as part of a universal machine. This model has independent rise and fall adjustment whereas most others are linked to the thicknessing bed of the planer for vertical table height adjustment. (Photo: courtesy Startrite Machinery Ltd., Gillingham.)

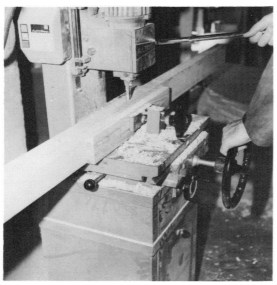

cutting, or milling action so that they can be traversed to mill a slot. The bit should not be subjected to excessive side loads and rule of thumb operation is to plunge the bit to a depth roughly equivalent to its own diameter (i.e. plunge a 9 mm ($\frac{3}{8}''$) diameter bit to a depth of 9 mm ($\frac{3}{8}''$)) then traverse, plunge again to a similar depth, traverse, and so on until the slot has been milled to its full depth and length. The potential side loading on any milling cutter restricts its overall length and in the case of wood mortising bits this rarely exceeds 50 mm (2") for a 12 mm ($\frac{1}{2}''$) diameter bit and proportionately less for thinner bits.

Peripheral speeds of mortising bits are much lower than is the case with most other wood machine cutting tools. Driven speeds are in the region of 6000 rpm and bit diameter range from about 6 mm–21 mm ($\frac{1}{4}''$ to $\frac{7}{8}''$). The consequence of this is that single or twin fluted milling bits have a very considerable "bite". They should not, therefore, be used in hand-fed workpiece machining and the workpiece must always be firmly clamped to the worktable before it meets the bit. For the same reason, machine milling bits of this pattern should not be used in hand drills. (Milling or side-cutting bits are available for free-hand use but these have a far greater number of cutting edges. This limits the bite that can be taken by each individual edge and minimizes the tendency of the cutter to snatch at unclamped work.)

Hollow Chisel Mortisers are the traditional mortising machines found in virtually all small and medium size British joinery shops. Strangely, these are much less common on the Continent where heavy duty slot, chain or oscillating chisel mortisers are much more common. Certainly in terms of capital outlay the hollow chisel mortiser provides the least expensive and most readily available method of preparing the deep rectangular mortises of widely differing size necessary for many joinery projects.

Figure 119 shows a typical, British-made hollow chisel mortiser. The two part cutting tool is comprised of a rotating wood auger directly mounted and driven in a motor shaft chuck. The auger is encased in a clamped hollow square chisel and the complete motor/tool assembly is plunged vertically downwards to enter the workpiece. The auger acts in the conventional way to drill a hole while the sharp cutting wings of the closely following chisel shear four corners to the hole by guillotine action. The result is a

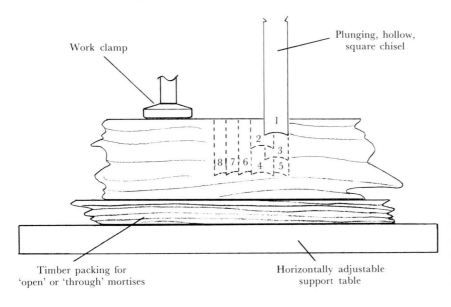

Work clamp

Plunging, hollow, square chisel

Timber packing for 'open' or 'through' mortises

Horizontally adjustable support table

Fig. 122 Large rectangular mortises will generally have to be chopped in stages to avoid chisel clogging and excessive strain on the machine components.

square hole. The tool is then withdrawn, the work traversed and the mortise elongated by successive plunge actions. Depending on the density of the timber and the size of chisel used, it may not be possible to complete a plunge action to the full depth of mortise set on the adjustable depth stop. This occurs specifically when working with the larger section chisels on hardwoods. In such cases the chisel is plunged into the workpiece until the leverage needed to continue the plunge action becomes excessive. The chisel is then withdrawn and the work traversed under the plunge line for a distance roughly equivalent to half the chisel width (i.e in the case of a 12 mm ($\frac{1}{2}''$) chisel the work would be traversed for approximately 6 mm ($\frac{1}{4}''$). A second plunge can then be taken until similar resistance is felt, the chisel again withdrawn, the work repositioned to its original setting against the end stop where a third plunge is taken, and so on until the full depth of the required mortise is achieved. The remainder of the mortise is chopped out with a succession of full plunges using half the chisel width. (Fig. 122.)

Chisel/auger clearance is critical to the successful operation of this tool and the actual clearance necessary between the upper faces of the auger wings and internal faces of the chisel mouth is about a coin thickness. If the clearance at this point is insufficient, the tool will quickly overheat due to the compression of waste chips as they are drawn up and squeezed through this gap. On the other hand, if working clearance is excessive, then chips may be too large to be readily ejected through the chisel slot and consequent compaction of waste inside the chisel will jam the auger or break it. Clearance can be set as shown in Fig. 123.

(c) (right) The yoke is now slackened, the coin removed and the chisel slid up finally into the yoke and re-clamped. The clearance which was afforded by the coin between the chisel shoulder and yoke has now been transferred to the mouth of the chisel between itself and the auger.

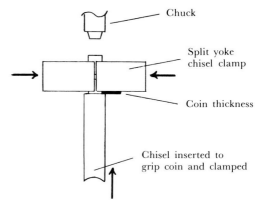

Fig. 123(a) The chisel is inserted into the split yoke and a coin gripped between the flat shoulder of the chisel and the lower face of the yoke.

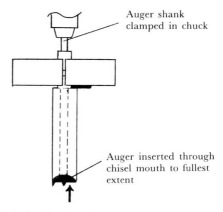

(b) With the chisel still firmly clamped in the yoke, the auger is inserted through the chisel mouth until the upper faces of the auger wings make contact and no further entry of the auger is possible. At this point the auger shank is clamped in the chuck.

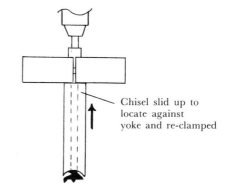

Chain Mortisers operate on much the same principle as a chain saw with a sprocket-driven cutting chain tracking around a chain bar and sprocket nose. In appearance and operation it is similar to the hollow chisel mortiser but in this case the motor is mounted horizontally with a chain sprocket fitted to its shaft and, on entry into the workpiece, a rectangular mortise is cut in one operation. Chain and bar assemblies are available in a wide variety of section sizes to chop mortises of virtually any useful size in one or two head plunges. This obviously saves a great deal of production time but it has to be remembered that the bottom of the mortise will be radiused and therefore only suitable for "open" mortise joints (i.e. mortises which are cut right through the workpiece) or for deep, blind mortising – "deep" in this instance meaning in relation to the section size of the tenon. An important component of the chain mortiser is the chip breaker. This is generally of a hardwood such as beech and serves to prevent splintering of the workpiece at the point where the chain emerges from it. An alternative to this is a chip breaking lath which acts in the same manner as a spelching fence or block. In this case a lath of scrap timber is clamped on top of the workpiece prior to mortising and the chain breaks out of and causes splintering to the lath rather than the workpiece. (Fig. 125.)

Machines such as the chain mortiser are generally found in larger joinery shops and as such may be in more or less continuous use. It is important that work is not left clamped in position on the worktable overnight, or, if it is, the security of the clamps must be checked before machining operations are recommenced the following morning. Accidents occurring at start-up time are frequently as a result of clamped work-in-progress having moved during the preceding sixteen hours.

Fig. 124 A typical chain mortiser (telescopic guard retracted). This machine also has a second plunging head on the right for a hollow square chisel.

Guards are provided to completely shroud the chain above the work and must always be in place when the machine is running. (Photo: courtesy L.R. Flacke & Co., Cardiff.)

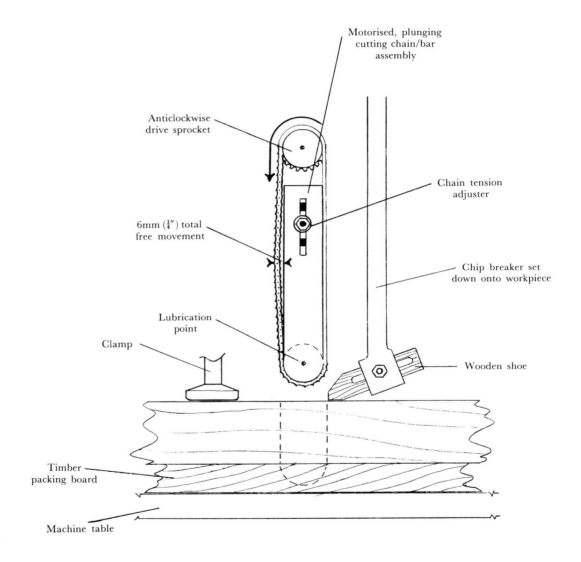

Motorised, plunging
cutting chain/bar
assembly

Anticlockwise
drive sprocket

Chain tension
adjuster

6mm ($\frac{1}{4}''$) total
free movement

Chip breaker set
down onto workpiece

Lubrication
point

Clamp

Wooden shoe

Timber
packing board

Machine table

Fig. 125 The chip breaking shoe is locked down onto the workpiece at the chain's exit point. To elongate a mortise the head should be withdrawn after the initial plunge, the clamped work/table assembly traversed to the required position, a second plunge made, and so on.

Note: *The cutter head guard which totally encloses the chain assembly must always be used and locked within 12mm ($\frac{1}{2}''$) of the work surface.*

116

Oscillating Mortisers chop rectangular mortises with flat bottoms in the fastest time possible and are found almost exclusively in production line environments. Two chisels chop into the clamped workpiece at the lateral extremities of the mortise while the double cutting action waste clearance tool oscillates between them. Hopper feed and fully automatic "tape" control are the norm for these machines. The tool changing and setting time is considerably longer than for other types of mortiser. This fact and its capital cost make the oscillating chisel mortiser the least useful for one-off and short run jobs. (Fig. 126.)

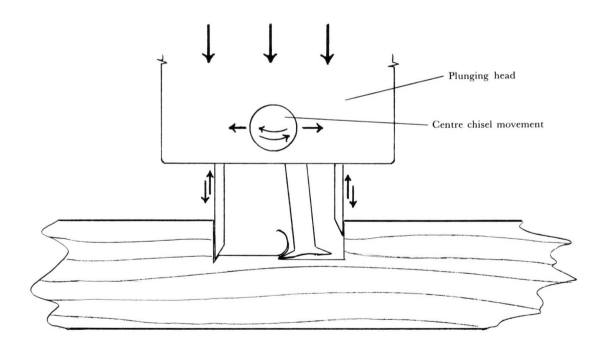

Plunging head

Centre chisel movement

Fig. 126 Oscillating mortiser: The two chisels at either end of the mortise work with a reciprocating pump action while the two wing centre chisel moves back and fore between them to pare away the waste. The whole motorised head assembly is plunged progressively into the workpiece.

This type of mortiser is designed to work horizontally (i.e. the above illustration is as seen from above) which has some advantages when edge mortising and also aids chip clearance.

Tenoners

Single End Tenoners are those which cut a tenon on one end of the workpiece only in a single operation. Design varies considerably across the price range but the model shown in Figure 127 is, in my opinion, the most useful and least expensive pattern for continuously varied production. The fact that both cutting heads are mounted on *vertical* shafts, one to cut the top face of the tenon and one the bottom, means that "scribing" (i.e., in this context, undercut shoulders or counter-profiles being referred to as "scribes") cutterheads can be used, if required, to match the cross section profile of the components being jointed. Two motorized cutterheads suffice, therefore, where three, four or even five heads (one being a lengthing saw) are utilized in other designs. Combinations of 90 degree and bevelled cutting discs with appropriate spacers can also be fitted to the tenoner for the purpose of producing the "open" or interleaved tenon joints commonly used in sash frame construction.

Fig. 127 An economical single-end tenoner. The upper and lower heads are vertically and horizontally adjustable. Tool stacks for open sash joints can also be fitted. (Photo: courtesy Multico Ltd., Redhill, Surrey.)

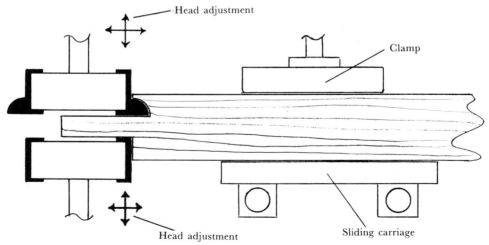

Fig. 128 Eye-level view of the in-feed side of the single-end tenoner (i.e. the sliding table is travelling directly away from the observer).

Where versatility and economy are prime considerations the Multico version of this machine meets every need with the added advantage that it can be converted for single-pass, double-end tenoning. Maximum tenon length which can be cut in a single pass is 127mm (5") or 230mm (9") in two passes.

118

Double End Tenoners are those used for tenoning both ends of a rail simultaneously. This, at the very least, halves production time and is therefore worth evaluating in any production circumstances where high output of identical components at minimum cost is projected. The machine itself is essentially a left-hand single-end tenoner and right-hand single-end tenoner married by a rigid frame with rails which allows one of both of the composite heads to be moved and locked at a pre-set distance from each other. The unit shown in Figure 129 has all the capital economy advantages of the single-end version described previously, in that scribing and off-setting of shoulders to allow for rebates, etc., can be provided with the minimum of tool-setting experience and consequent cost.

Fig. 129 The Multico single-end tenoner can also be converted to a double-end unit for simultaneous machining of workpiece ends. (Photo: courtesy Multico Ltd., Redhill, Surrey.)

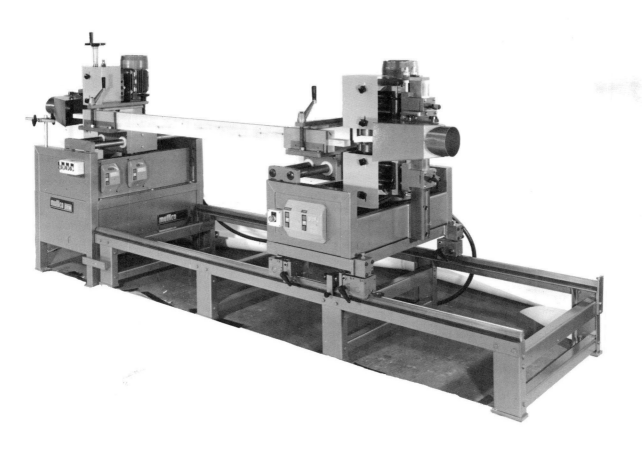

Routers

The modern machine router was inspired by the need to mechanize hand routing (principally, the grooving of work faces) with a tooth plane. Having developed the exceptionally high-speed shafts necessary to achieve adequate peripheral speeds on narrow diameter rotary cutting bits, many more uses were found for the tool. Nowadays, particularly with the introduction of man-made boards and laminates, a portable power tool version of the router will be found invaluable in any wood workshop. Power tools have one significant advantage over floor standing machines in that they can be taken to the work. The size of the work therefore becomes irrelevant and workpieces too large to be offered safely to machine heads by hand feed can be worked successfully.

It should be remembered that all the basic principles of operation and forces at work in respect of rotating machine cutters as discussed through the preceding chapters apply equally to rotary cutting, hand-held power tools. Although the rotating masses and consequent energies developed will generally be less than for equivalent machines, safety and tool performance both demand attention to these principles. Feeding the tool *against* the direction of cutter rotation, for example, so that the cutter force is *opposing* the forward feed of the tool rather than assisting it is as vital in the case of a hand held portable power saw as the rule of feeding *against* the direction of cutter rotation on a conventional sawbench.

The overhead machine router is used extensively in modern workshops (if not almost exclusively), for production shaping and finishing work on man-made boards and sheet materials. It has an advantage over any other combination of machines for this purpose in that it will cut and finish a thin workpiece edge of almost any contour in a single and extremely precise operation. Such machines are generally used with templates and/or work holding or feeding jigs. This of course is essential for efficiency in repetition work.

Portable routers can be mounted in the inverted position with the tool-holding collet projecting through a bench aperture. With provision of a split fence or by using router cutters with "pilot" noses or ball bearings, the router then becomes a miniature version of the spindle moulder.

I am often asked if, in fact, an inverted router can be used as a substitute for a spindle moulder. The straight answer is, no. A router can do some of the jobs normally done by a spindle moulder, but realistically, these are restricted to the lightest of simple moulding operations. To machine a 25 mm ($1''$) $\times$ 37 mm ($1\frac{1}{2}''$) rebate, for example, would require about six separate feeds over an inverted router with fence and cutter height setting alterations between each pass. The same operation could be carried out in a single pass across the average vertical spindle moulder. Deep or compound mouldings would similarly have to be machined in a succession of passes, rarely removing more than about 12 mm ($\frac{1}{2}''$) square section of timber at any one time. Mouldings produced in this way will additionally, inevitably, require hand finishing to remove unwanted linear machine marks. None of this is to say that such operations *cannot* be carried out – they cannot be carried out *well*.

Machine routers (and bench drills) must always be fitted with a telescopically adjustable guard to shroud the chuck and non-working part of the cutter. Most portable routers on the other hand are now of the plunging type and their construction is such that, both from considerations of visibility and waste clearance, effective guarding above the sole plate would be difficult to provide, although the regulations demand that all moving parts must be enclosed 'so far as is practicable'. In practice, both the operator's hands are necessarily holding the handles at either side of the motor to control and guide the tool. Provided single handed operation is not attempted (perhaps when one hand is *wrongly* used to support or steady the workpiece) then both hands will be out of reach of the cutter. General rules of operation are the same as for any other machine but particular attention should be given to securing small workpieces adequately before attempting to machine them. Also, eye protection should always be provided in the form of safety spectacles, goggles or face shield.

Fig. 130 A machine router. Note the cutter guard and the use of a work-holding jig. (Photo: courtesy Wadkin, Leicester.)

Drills

Some means of drilling holes for screw fixed assemblies, dowel jointing, etc., is an obvious necessity in any workshop. The simplest drilling tools are hand drills, either manual or powered but such tools require a high and consistent degree of operator skill where the holes produced play a part in component alignment. Here, drilling is not simply a matter of centring but also precise angular introduction. It will be the case that many existing workshop machines already incorporate, or can be fitted with, drill chucks, (e.g., mortisers, radial arm saws, lathes and some circular saws). These are useful for some work – particularly horizontal drilling and boring – but are generally restricted to 90 degree introduction unless special work-holding jigs or tables are made to allow for angled presentation of the workpiece. A bench drill (or drill press) is the most practical machine for meeting these needs.

Engineers coming into woodworking will be altogether happier people if they can revise their definition of "working tolerance" (i.e. the measurement of acceptable inaccuracy). "Near enough" by eye may be a difficult frame of reference for purists to adopt but it is a realistic one in woodworking terminology. (This is still a long way short of the "... ask yourself what it would look like through the bottom of a glass at one o'clock on New Year's Eve" approach to the subject of working tolerance.) With this in mind, a bench drill that would not be acceptable for tool room use will be very useful in the wood workshop.

Sanders

Many sanding jobs can be effectively carried out by hand or machines which simulate hand sanding. These are the sort of jobs which involve removing the smallest amounts of timber such as odd whiskers, local end-grain problems, minimal machine marks (which although virtually invisible on untreated timber are highlighted under a varnish coat), workpieces either too small or too large to be offered to the machines available, etc. In all such cases sanding should be kept to the minimum necessary as no actual change of component shape or dimension is required. Heavier sanding jobs, such as those where a reduction of surface levels is required, (e.g. across face joints, etc.) will require the speed and accuracy provided with machine sanders.

A point to note in regard to all sanding jobs is that it should not be a substitute for clean and accurate machining.

Whatever the type of machine sander used, a little understanding of the nature of the abrasive material itself will be helpful in obtaining the best performance. The sharp grit particles which abrade or cut away the timber being sanded are graded according to size. The grade numbers refer to nominal particle size in fractions of an inch. "80 grit" would therefore have grit particles measuring approximately one eightieth of an inch across; "150 grit", one hundred and fiftieth of an inch across and so on. High grit numbers, therefore, refer to fine abrasives and low grit numbers to coarser qualities. Whether hand or machine sanding, always try to start the job with a grade of paper near the grade that will be required for finishing. Scoring left in a workface by a coarse grit paper will have to be removed by progressive use of lighter grits. For example, if the job is in pine and is perhaps a piece of furniture rather than joinery, you may decide that face finishing will be satisfactory with 120 or 150 grit paper. If the machining has been good, it may well be feasible to start and finish the sanding with the actual finishing grit. Otherwise, initial coarse sanding should be carried out with a grade within 20 to 50 grit sizes of it.

It is important that face timbers are always sanded *with* the grain to avoid cross-grain scratching. Where cross-grain sanding is unavoidable (mitred corners, "T" joints, etc.), the finest grit possible should be used to minimize the problem. Once such scratching has occurred, it may be almost impossible to remove all traces of it without actually reducing the surface level by a noticeable degree. Hand-held sanders of the "orbital" type are most helpful for general fine finishing of multi-directional grain faces.

Fig. 131 Sanders can be used for very accurate finishing, shaping and dimensioning of many workpieces which, in a small workshop, cannot economically be produced in any other way. This machine has unique tilting and swivelling facilities that makes it amongst the most useful of sanding units. (Photo: courtesy Luna Tools & Machinery Ltd., Milton Keynes.)

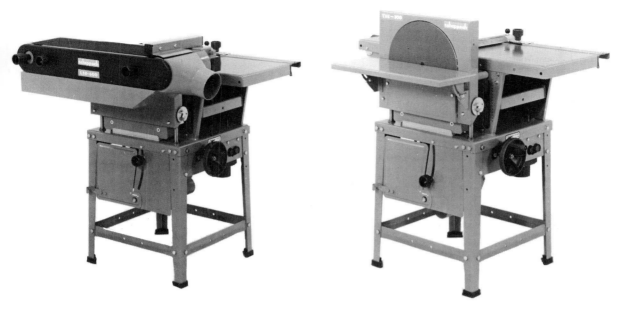

Fig. 132(a) Independent disc and belt (linishing) sanders are not produced by many manufacturers at a cost attractive to small workshop users. Either of these heads may, however, be available as an attachment for another machine such as this planer/thicknesser. (Photo: courtesy Sumaco Ltd., Elland, Yorks.)

Application of excessive pressure to "speed" the sanding process should be avoided. In fact the abrasive will work *better* and *longer* if minimal pressure is used. A heavy hand on sanders results in heat generation on the work face and "burning" and clogging rather than cool cutting. This applies to every type of sanding machine.

"Belt" sanders are the best for sanding surfaces uniformly *with* the general run of the grain. The "Linisher" is a belt sander with a rigid bed over which the belt runs. Work components are then taken to the machine and sanded. This, of course, means that it is the workpiece which is being held, freehand, and some care is necessary to ensure that even pressure is applied along the length of the piece. For this reason the linisher is generally reserved for reducing projections on edges and the like. In a small workshop, however, it will be found very useful for more general sanding duties and freehand shaping using the linishing bed for straight or convex faces and edges and the exposed end-drum or driving belt pulley for concave contours. Because of the ease with which a true edge or face can be destroyed on a belt sander of this type, linishers are generally fitted with comparitively fine grit belts.

Overhead belt sanders are rarely found in small workshops due to their size and consequent space demands, not to mention their cost in relation to likely work loading. Even so, where space and cash can be found, they are the most useful machine sander for general work. Two examples of this machine are illustrated. Both have the advantage that large components and/or assemblies can be laid on a work support table and sanded over the whole face area with hand pressure alone.

"Disc" sanders are the most versatile and accurate for general end-grain sanding and face sanding where radial scratching may be hidden or not matter. Their advantage for

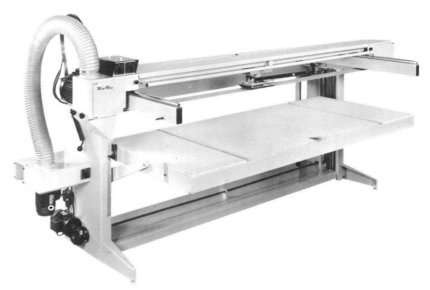

Fig. 133 A large belt sander such as this is invaluable in general joinery. The unit shown has power rise and fall to the work support table and another useful feature is that the table tilts vertically so that large work can be clamped to it for edge as well as face sanding. The beam support arms also fold back so that the machine occupies very little space when not in use. (Photo: courtesy Luna Tools & Machinery, Milton Keynes.)

Fig. 134 On some sanders the upper run of the belt is accessible for linishing. On this model the beam also tilts down so that the linishing surface is at 90° to the work support table for edge sanding. For conventional pad sanding the table is set at a height appropriate to the work thickness and pulled back and fore whilst pressure is applied through a pad to bring the belt into contact with the work. (Model: Luna YK1500). (Photo: courtesy J. Fox & Sons, Cardiff.)

extremely accurate dimensioning lies in the fact that the abrasive disc is firmly fixed to its backing plate. Used with angle jigs or a back-fence (see "Spindle Moulder") it can therefore be used for shaping or finishing small components to a tolerance not realistically feasible with other linear or rotary cutting machines or sanders.

"Speed" sanders are power fed production machines used for finish sanding wide panels, table tops etc. in one fast operation. They can also, of course, be used for sanding smaller individual timber components prior to their assembly. The workpiece is carried into the machine on a rubberized conveyor belt type bed and passes under two or three abrasive drums or belts of progressively finer grit size. The height of the bed is adjustable so that the final thickness of the stock is controlled.

No particular safety precautions – other than those relative to the use of all machines – are uniquely applicable to the use of overhead (or pad) sanders. A point that should be borne in mind, however, is that a broken belt can cause injury if it is allowed to fly from the machine. Those models of pad sander which give access to the upper run of the belt for linishing should, therefore, have a beam guard for covering this section when not in use.

Note: One major concern with the installation of any machine sanding unit is dust extraction. Extensive regulations governing motor types and waste storage enclosures are in force for all production machines and for high capacity sanders these are particularly stringent. The dangers associated with sanding dust relate not only to longer term health damage as a result of regularly inhaling fine dust particles (some timbers actually produce toxic dust), but also in fire and spontaneous explosion risks which are very real once the floating dust/air mix reaches a critical saturation.

These considerations apart however, for small workshops where sanding is likely to be an intermittent activity, obvious safeguards

are to wear a dust mask and ensure that as much fresh air ventilation as possible is provided to prevent excessive build-up of free dust in the workshop atmosphere. (See also Chapter 11 "Waste Extraction".)

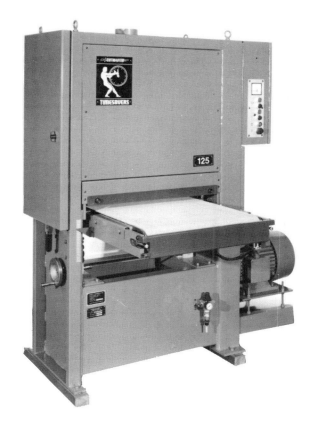

Fig. 135 A "speed" sander. (Photo: courtesy Thomas White & Sons, Cleckheaton, W. Yorks.)

CHAPTER NINE

Universals

A single machine combining several heads to carry out many of the principal woodmachining functions may be an attractive proposition for the smaller workshop. It certainly can save space and cash. Advertisers often, however, make a great deal out of very little and the *real* value of any particular unit can be obscured. Even a simple sawbench for example can be presented as: "A *ten function* machine for your workshop! ... It rips, crosscuts, bevels, grooves, mitres, chamfers, tenons, rebates, cuts compound angles in hard or softwood ...", and so on. With the addition of a power take-off, the list can be almost endless. Direct comparison of machines on this basis is obviously misleading. Of course, the sawbench will do all these things, but in the business of comparing and evaluating options it is most beneficial to concentrate on the *principal* machining functions in their most basic form and which are central to the major proportion of all general workshop output. The list of functions below has been drawn up on this basis and ignores the fact that some saws may be used for moulding, some planers may be used for tenoning, some moulders may be used for sawing, etc. Improvisation and/or the use of attachments can extend the usefulness of many machines but this is best regarded as a possible bonus rather than a prime objective. The machines which will do each job best are the machines which have been specifically designed for that job.

Function	Machine
Sawing	Circular saw
	Bandsaw
	Radial Arm saw
Surface planing	Surface Planer
Thicknessing	Thicknesser
Moulding	Spindle Moulder
Turning	Lathe

For the purposes of simplification in this section I have omitted mortising and tenoning. Many universal machines include or offer a slot mortiser driven from the planer block. Hollow chisel mortising adaptors are available for some of these and are effective for limited production of small mortises but are no substitute for the free standing chisel mortiser (described in the previous chapter) used for general joinery. Similarly, tenoning can be carried out on one of the saws or on a suitably tooled spindle moulder. For production on a larger scale, again, particularly for joinery, a purpose-built tenoner, such as the 'Multico' machine, will be found by far the most economical.

Of the functions and machines listed above, no manufacturer has, as yet, managed to combine these units successfully – "successfully" meaning without real loss of working convenience and efficiency. Nor is it strictly necessary to have a machine for every function. Remember that many operations can be carried out very well with hand tools cheaply;

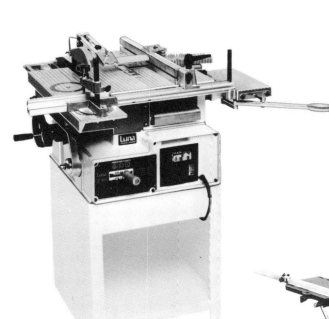

Fig. 136(a) (left) A low cost, compact version of the universal systems which incorporate sawing, planning, thicknessing, moulding and mortising heads together with a sliding carriage serving the saw and spindle. (Photo: courtesy Luna Tools & Machinery Ltd., Milton Keynes.)

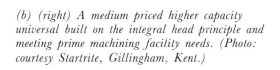

(b) (right) A medium priced higher capacity universal built on the integral head principle and meeting prime machining facility needs. (Photo: courtesy Startrite, Gillingham, Kent.)

(c) (left) Near the top end of the range of universals built on this principle is the Luna W59. It incorporates a tilt arbor saw with 100mm (4″) cut at 90°; a 3 speed moulder with nearly 125mm (5″) vertical adjustment; a long-bed surface planer with cast, tilting fence; a 254 × 230mm (10″ × 9″) thicknesser and a slot mortiser that can be adapted for hollow chisel mortising. For business users it is also useful to know that the machine can be simply coverted into an independent saw/spindle and separate planer/thicknesser/mortiser if required. The W59 is also available with planer/thicknesser section up to 400 × 230mm (16″ × 9″). (Photo: courtesy Luna Tools & Machinery Ltd., Milton Keynes.)

Fig. 137(a) The Scheppach universal system is representative of the best of its type as all the principal machining requirements are catered for. The photographs show the basic planer/thicknesser unit with three different machine head attachments fitted. Changeover times for complete removal of one attachment and fitting of another average around two to three minutes once familiarity with the mechanics has been gained. In addition to the saw, spindle and mortising attachments shown, a bandsaw, belt sander, disc sander, rustic brushing, grinding and lathe attachment are offered. (Photo: courtesy Sumaco, Elland, Yorks.)

Fig. 137(c)

other operations will be called for very frequently and are therefore best mechanized. One of the saws and a planer/thicknesser, for example, will be in almost constant use whereas other units may be idle for days or weeks. When working on a limited budget therefore, it is unwise to sacrifice performance and quality in an important machine such as a saw, simply so that other equipment can be included for the same total outlay. It will often be better to settle for having to do some of the less frequently called for operations by hand and not experience the frustrations of working with machines which are used for 90% of production time and which do not perform their *basic* functions efficiently. (It will matter little to you that your sawbench has an attachment for stripping wallpaper when you have been struggling to make it saw to a line or at 90°.)

To this end, where a universal machine is decided upon, I would advise the buyer to concentrate on the most frequently used functions and not be distracted by gimmicks or "features" which have little practical value. One choice would be for a universal of the type shown in Figure 136 which combines a sawbench and spindle moulder sharing the same sliding carriage, a planer/thicknesser and generally a slot mortiser. The other functions would be catered for with separate, independent machines; a bandsaw for deep cutting and general shaping; a radial arm saw for heavy (and light) crosscutting and a lathe for woodturning.

An entirely different approach to the "which universal" question is shown in the photos (Fig. 137) of the 'Scheppach' system. Here, the basic, floor standing unit is a 10″ × 6″ planer/thicknesser to which complete machine head/table attachments are fitted. Some time in function changing is lost in this design but this may be outweighed in some instances by its comparatively large capacities for a universal in this price bracket. A further possible benefit is that attachments can be purchased specifically in line with actual need and over a period of time. Attachments include a saw table, spindle moulder, slot mortiser, lathe (I would personally always opt for an independent lathe if at all possible for reasons explained in the chapter on woodturning) and a bandsaw.

Yet another approach to the universal concept is shown in the 'Kity' system. This is essentially a selection of independent machines mounted on a common table and driven from a central motor. Changing from one operation to another is by belt change and takes less time than the interchange of complete attachments necessary with the 'Scheppach' system. On the other hand, the floor and working space requirements of the comparable 'Kity' system are considerably greater. Again, a bandsaw can be included in the machine head selection, but this is mounted in the place normally occupied by the circular saw and complete interchange is necessary if both units are to be included. As with all the universals so far described, the functions of a radial arm saw are not catered for within the system. (Fig. 138.)

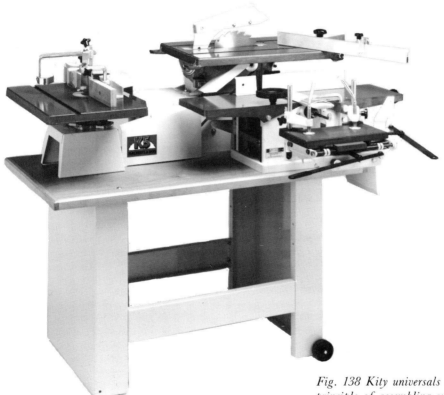

Fig. 138 Kity universals are built on the principle of assembling what are essentially independent machines on a common base to be driven from a centrally positioned motor. Manual belt transferral takes no more than a few seconds. The smaller of the two machines (the K5 illustrated) will be of particular interest to home woodworkers. A larger version is now available with electronic, push button function changing and each of the three principal heads (saw, spindle and planer/thicknesser) can be converted for independent use. (Photo: courtesy Kity U.K., Shipley, W. Yorks.)

One system that has fairly recently been introduced to the U.K. from America is the "Shopsmith". This is basically a lathe with variable speed main shaft and to which attachments can be fitted on the left or right. The headstock slides along twin bed bars to vary the centre capacity of the lathe or to position if for one of its alternative modes. The bed/headstock assembly hinges to the vertical from the tailstock end for use as a drill press or vertical shaft for routing and moulding accessories. Other functions within the standard specification include circular sawing and disc sanding. A moulding block can be fitted and used also in the horizontal position. Machine attachments for the power take-off on the left of the headstock include a surface planer (no thicknesser), bandsaw, fretsaw and belt sander. (Fig. 139.)

Other designs of universals are available and no doubt others will be developed. Specific references as to current limitations imposed by a particular design may therefore be inapplicable as you read this book. The four types described are simply representative of the universals which meet the principal criteria for such systems in that they are built around, or include, the basic functions essential to general output.

Advice on operating procedures for each machine head included in a universal system is the same as for the independent machine covered in the relevant chapter.

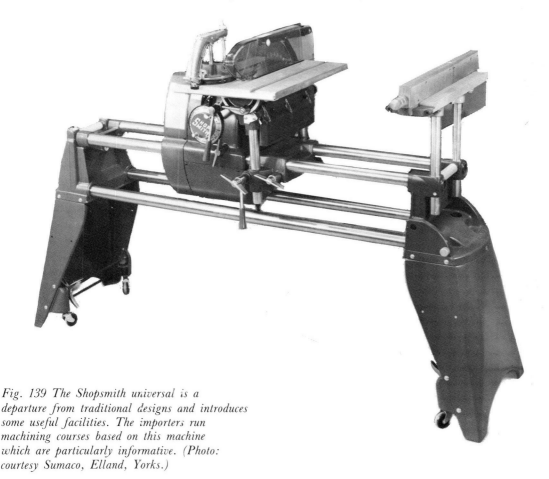

Fig. 139 The Shopsmith universal is a departure from traditional designs and introduces some useful facilities. The importers run machining courses based on this machine which are particularly informative. (Photo: courtesy Sumaco, Elland, Yorks.)

CHAPTER TEN

General Health & Safety

Guarding:

It may well be that you do not have to comply with any statutory regulations in relation to machine guarding but this is obviously no reason to ignore these rules. In the main, such regulations have been framed as a direct result of common accidents and such accidents now rarely occur when proper guarding and operating procedures are observed. For example, all parts of a cutter assembly which are not necessarily exposed for the machining operation must be guarded so that it is not possible for you, or anyone visiting your workshop to make accidental contact with the cutters. Concentration is rightly focused on the feed path of a workpiece during machining and it *is* highly dangerous to be working near any unguarded cutter which is not directly involved in the operation. Parts of a machine not in the feed path tend to be used casually for leaning on, storage of push blocks, etc. necessary for a feed, and so on.

Even though the law may not require it then, it is most definitely in everyone's interests that guarding be understood and applied. If anything, this may be more important in a home workshop than a professional one where at least the operator and those likely to be in the vicinity of the machine are used to working with machinery and will be familiar with the dangers. Home workshops tend to be more cluttered and every available surface is often called into service at some time for supporting something, be it a box of screws or a cup of tea and a plate of biscuits brought in for the worker by someone who knows nothing whatsoever about woodworking machinery.

Most machines are supplied with all necessary guards and it is always worth taking the time to see that they are properly fitted. If guards are not available then the machine should not be used until some have been made and securely fitted.

It is not only rotating or linear cutters which can cause problems. Drive belts, rotating chucks (particularly those at low level such as the horizontal mortising chuck on many planers), gears and pulley wheels, must all be guarded so that it is not possible for a finger or maybe a loose cuff to become trapped. Again, if for any reason such guards or enclosures are not fitted, the few hours that may be required to make the machine safe are hours well spent and will make your machining an altogether more relaxing and enjoyable business. Your entire concentration can be directed to the job in hand.

Readers in the U.S.A. and other countries will have similar standards and ratings to ensure the safety of operators and others in the vicinity.

Eye Protection:

The most common category of injury is that affecting the eyes. Fortunately most of these accidents are not serious but of course they are always painful, and the mere fact that some unexpected particle of machine waste can hit the operator's eye is an indication that protection is needed. Any eye injury is potentially very serious indeed and yet can be simply avoided.

Undoubtedly, we have an illogical resistance to adopting many common sense safety measures, such as the wearing of seat belts before we were made to, if we feel that our freedom to choose is being interfered with, or by inference, perhaps, that we will be regarded as over-cautious or not in total control of the circumstances in which we are operating. Ordinary glasses are not conspicuous in this regard and do give a good measure of protection against small particles which come at the eye directly. If they are worn in actual anticipation of this problem, however, there is a good case for having the standard lenses replaced with toughened or laminated ones. Best of all will be proper safety goggles or, if you find these uncomfortable for prolonged wear, safety spectacles. These give a very high degree of all-round protection, will not mist up and, provided they have the British Standards mark, will stop a "grade two" impact. This is defined as a $\frac{1}{4}''$ diameter steel ball fired at a velocity of $150'$ per second – about the peripheral speed of a circular saw. Some operations, such as those carried out at grinding wheels, require that the operator wears eye protection which will resist a "Grade 1" impact (greater than grade 2), and this will probably mean that appropriate goggles or a full face shield will have to be worn under the regulatory requirements as, at the time of writing, no safety spectacles are made to this standard. (The potential danger in the particular case of grinding wheels does not, of course, arise from simple grinding dust or sparks, but rather the possibility of a wheel itself disintegrating.)

Dust Filtration:

Probably the majority of small workshops do not have dust extraction equipment, or do have a mobile extractor which is being used to extract waste from one machine when it is needed on another. Also, unless the extractor is perfectly sited when trying to extract from machines which discharge a large proportion of their waste into the open air (sanding work mounted in a lathe for example), then much of the dust will miss the suction inlet or hood.

A face mask which covers the nose and mouth at such times may be a little uncomfortable to wear but is still preferable to inhaling heavy concentrations of floating dust over the same period of time. A dust mask with replaceable filter pads or disposable paper filter masks should be on hand in every wood machine shop. (See also Chapter 11.)

Ear Protection:

Damage to hearing through exposure to continuous loud noise is generally a slow process but irreversible. Fortunately, there should be few occasions in small workshops when noise levels are such or of sufficient duration that ear defenders are needed. There are occasions, however, say, when using the thicknesser for processing a whole batch of components that might take a day, when the case for wearing ear protectors is a good one. At the end of such a day, the sheer pleasure and physical relief experienced in the sudden absence of noise is an indication of the pressure it has added without us being directly aware of it. Headaches and general tension can often be traced to such factors.

Most of the machines that have been discussed in this book and likely to be found in home or light commercial use are not particularly noisy. Most of the noise they do make is caused by the movement of cutters through the air rather than gears meshing, etc., and as virtually all of these machines have circular cutters and blocks their free running noise is quite acceptable. (Blunt cutters will add considerably to operational noise level.) Also, apart from the lathe which should run with very little noise, although for long periods, the other workshop machines tend to be used intermittently. Power tools on the other hand, particularly used in confined spaces, make a great deal of noise, and if they are to be used for prolonged periods, ear defenders should be worn.

The subject of noise in industrial workshops is one covered by a great deal of legislation involving the use of noise-reducing cutters, workpiece damping, acoustic enclosures and so on, and its importance should be recognised.

Because large production shops are governed by statute in this regard it is unusual to see any operator without ear protectors nowadays. Here, huge multi-cutter machines carrying massive square cutter-blocks are running from first to last thing and buffet the air continuously in a way that can actually cause physical pain. Even before the advent of today's legislation and the general availability of ear protectors many machinists sensibly chose to use cotton wool or cloth plugs, although neither material is used in the manufacture of ear plugs or protectors which are acceptable under current legislation.

As with all the items mentioned in this chapter the cost of ear protectors is minimal and having them available for the odd occasions when they might be needed is worthwhile.

Fire Risks:

Prevention is better than cure, but if a fire does start a clear idea of how to deal with it is essential. Water is useful for a limited range of burning materials but it is surprising how much of it is needed. It is also surprising how long it can take to find a bucket and even more surprising how long it can take to fill when held sideways under a wash-basin tap. A fire extinguisher suitable for dealing with electrical and chemical fires (inflammable sealers etc.) seems to be worth every bit of its cost at such times.

Frayed or overloaded cables and wiring are common causes of fire and from this point of view alone should be inspected regularly and replaced where necessary. Accumulations of dust on switchgear should also be avoided and a regular clean-up of machine waste etc. will starve a fire of fuel that does get started. Inflammable liquids should be kept in a metal container and away from the main workshop area. Since I gave up smoking at the age of forty-two I would also make a "NO SMOKING" rule for the workshop. (Before I was forty-two I would have barely tolerated such an infringement on my rights. Now, I can see every good and sensible reason for it.)

First Aid:

As most of us keep some items of first aid equipment in the house, so too the workshop is an obvious place for such precautions to be taken. Small cuts, etc., can be washed and kept clean with sticking plaster. Larger injuries of this type should only be treated in the first instance by direct pressure over the wound to check bleeding. The most useful and essential item for this purpose is non-fluffy pad and bandage to keep it in place. "First Aid Kits" of the type usually available at the local chemist contain a lot of items that have limited usefulness when you have cut yourself – a selection of waterproof pimple plasters, a pair of scissors, "*Sal Volatile*" (whatever that is), assorted safety pins, a 1″ or 25 mm bandage, lemon wet-wipes, two sorts of cream for insect bites, a small card of thread, six aspirins and instructions for giving mouth-to-mouth resuscitation in five languages. No doubt the presence of all these items in the kit can be defended. My own feeling is, however, that the essential items of equipment can be bought specifically and much more cheaply.

Virtually every place of work is now required to comply with the regulations laid down under the "Health and Safety at Work" Act, whether or not that place would be considered a "factory" under other legislation. This means that if your workshop is anything other than a private, one-man, hobby-type workshop it is almost certain to be subject to these regulations and specific first-aid equipment related to the size of the place and the number of people using it, or having access to it, will be called for.

Lighting:

Natural light is the least tiring to work in and as much as possible should be introduced into the workshop. To supplement this on overcast days and winter evenings some form of artificial lighting will be needed. For general illumination flourescent tubes are cheap to run but many people find their light rather depressing. They can also have a stroboscopic effect when cutterhead cycles coincide, and a running cutter can appear to be stationary. Tungsten bulbs give a softer (kinder) light and the shadows created are quite helpful in getting a perspective on some kinds of work.

Over my own lathe I have a light on a long lead which enables me to move it to different ceiling hooks for various jobs. This is not because I could not add a further light; it is simply so that I do not have to work in my own shadow when working along the length of the bed or when standing at the end of the lathe for bowl work. In fact I find the light from a single 150 watt bulb to be adequate if it is properly positioned. Other lights may be necessary over other machines.

A free-standing anglepoise lamp will also be very useful.

Clothing:

Wear whatever is comfortable but avoid wearing a necktie which might hang down and become entangled in a chuck or picked up by a cutter. Similarly, loose cuffs must not be allowed to pass near any working machine head. A smock-type overall top has been adopted by many woodworkers over the years as a practical way of preventing any flap of clothing becoming a hazard and of course it has the added advantage of keeping everyday clothing clean of dust and chippings. The heavy cotton variety is slightly more expensive than the alternatives made from man-made fibres, but are more comfortable to wear particularly in warm or humid conditions. One manufacturer specializing in this type of garment is P. Lovell Workwear, 3 Heol Esgyn, Cardiff, CF2 6JT.

CHAPTER ELEVEN

Waste Extraction

Accumulations of waste around machines and fine dust in the atmosphere are an immediate and long-term health hazard to all woodworkers. Even so, an extraction system of any sort is generally one of the last pieces of equipment installed in growing workshops. This is understandable from the point of view that most workshops are run on a fairly tight budget and, in comparison with other machines' contributions to profit or output, a dust extractor seems to offer very little for a relatively large outlay.

Workshops where employees are at work, or to which the public have access, and, in some instances, even those used by a self-employed person, will be subject to the rules insisting on the provision of extraction equipment for certain types of machines. In woodworking, this means that virtually all machines used in a production environment *must* be connected to an extractor when working. A point worth remembering in this regard is that insurance cover on commercial premises may not protect the policy holder if it can be proved that machines were being used without proper extraction before a fire occurred. Whether this or any other single factor has influenced owners of small workshops seems doubtful when looking at the imbalance of machine to extractor sales. From my own experience, I would say that most woodworkers are eventually driven to acceptance of the need for an extractor by the impossibility of continuing work without one, rather than by pre-planning. Like many worth-while acquisitions, however, the full range of benefits an extraction system brings only become evident after its installation.

Most obvious of these is the convenience of not having to switch off a machine to clear production waste manually. But apart from piles of chips which impede access to the working area and which can become a hazard in their own right, machine performance itself suffers adversely once trapped waste builds up and begins to circulate in cutter housings. This problem is not confined to heavy production machines and users of "over and under" planer/thicknessers will have experienced the impracticability of continuing surfacing operations once waste on the thicknessing bed below reaches cutter-block height. The whole feel and performance of the machine changes perceptibly at this point and surface finish of the workpiece deteriorates rapidly as loose waste is carried around and impacted between the knives and work to damage the underlying fibres.

(Poking a stick into the thicknessing tunnel of a planer/thicknesser or the waste aperture of any working machine is a common but highly dangerous practice. Before any attempt is made to clear away accumulated waste, machines must *always* be switched off. Even then, waste should not be cleared from inside a cutter housing unless the machine has been isolated from the power supply. Many totally avoidable accidents have occurred through accidental start-up at such times trapping a limb or clothing close to cutters or power feed mechanisms. Whatever the inconvenience therefore, all machinists must make prior disconnection of any machine a golden rule before working on or near any exposed feed or cutter system.)

It must be admitted, of course, that machinery sited in a home workshop is likely to be used far less often and for shorter periods than professionally used equipment. Building a case for the introduction of an extraction system on grounds of efficiency and time saving alone in these circumstances may not be convincing. Tedious though it may be, collection and disposal of chip waste by hand is feasible and the user may be perfectly willing to accept less than optimum performance from some machines.

Chip waste is not, however, the only by-product of machining operations and the creation of fine particle waste is likely to be the problem which extraction is initially called on to solve. Hardwoods and man-made boards in particular break up into fine particles, not only when sanded but also under machine cutter action, and a high proportion of waste is produced in floating dust form. Such particles are a definite risk to health if breathed in regularly. In fact, some timbers (mainly from amongst imported, tropical species) give off toxic waste and unless prevented from entering the workshop atmosphere will cause severe irritation and, possibly, allergic reaction, to the mucous tissues lining the respiratory tracts and eyes. These effects are both immediately and cumulatively damaging.

In designing effective (and legal) extraction systems for the woodworking industry, waste is categorised as "chip" or "dust" and the requirements for collection systems for each are slightly different. Principally, the risk of explosion with a dust/air mix in an extractor is far greater than with a predominantly chip/air mix. Because of this the filter and collection components of a *dust* (as opposed to *chip*) extractor must be enclosed so as to prevent burning waste being blown into a working area in the event of an explosion. This is generally accomplished by enclosing the rel-evant parts of the system in a steel cabinet which must be vented to the atmosphere outside the workshop to provide escape (relief) for the explosive forces. An alternative is to have the unit enclosed by brick walls, or sited outside the workshop, but again, any enclosure must be vented to allow for the escape of expanding gases to the outside atmosphere.

Many woodworkers who may have thought that their mobile extractor was suited to the job of pulling waste from a sanding machine will have to think again in the light of this. In spite of my sincere wishes not to make life more difficult for fellow woodworkers, the requirements of the law are clear and justified by the unfortunate experiences of some who have tried to work outside it. In fact, it is not a difficult job to site any extractor permanently so that the consequences of a fire or explosion are minimized. One of the foremost considerations here will be the distance that waste has to be pulled from machine to extractor as efficiency drops as duct length increases. The following information will be of some help in making due allowance for this and other factors in designing a system suitable for a small workshop. Larger establishments will be well advised to consider the merits of calling in an extraction engineer for a comprehensive estimate of costs for a full system. The total may not be at all what was imagined and a full factory installation, such as that illustrated in Figure 140c, may cost little more than one of the dozen or so machines it will serve.

At the heart of any installation will be the motor and fan which pulls air through the ducts. These are rated on the volume of air they pull through the principal inlet duct, measured in terms of cubic feet per minute (cfm) or cubic metres per hour (m^3h). Not all manufacturers have adopted the same system of grading the performance of their machines and some anomalies are evident in comparisons between models which clearly cannot offer the claimed parity. This possibly arises because some manufacturers simply pass on the performance figures for the fan system without reference to the effects of enclosing it in its working environment. The suction capacity of any extractor should fairly be measured when it is set up as it will be when working – that is, with the filter and collection elements of the system in place. It is obvious that without this back-pressure from the waste delivery side of the system, air movement figures will be much greater (perhaps as much as 100 percent greater) than would normally be the case. Similarly, the performance of vacuum cleaner type extractors (where the collection bag also acts as the filter bag) will be progressively impaired to the point of uselessness as the bag fills and back-pressure increases.

Given that fan design in virtually all mobile and most stationary extractors follows the same principles and that meaningful variations only occur in size and proportional motor power, apparent differences in performance between basically similar models can be put down to variations in testing criteria. In other words, it can be fairly assumed that there will be little difference in the real performance of one three quarter horse power mobile extractor and another – whatever performance figures may imply to the contrary.

Performance figures in themselves are, of course, in any case, meaningless without experience of what they represent. As a general guide, a machine such as a 300 mm (12″) planer/thicknesser will need to be served by an extractor drawing around 350 cfm through a 100 mm (4″) diameter inlet. The air speed in the extraction duct of such an arrangement will be approximately 4000 feet per minute (fpm) which is the air speed recommended for chip waste extraction. From this it might be assumed that all mobile extractors rated at 600 cfm would be suitable for serving this machine *and* another, slightly smaller machine (through a smaller diameter duct in order to maintain the required air speed) simultaneously. Such is not the case and the fact that most "600 cfm" extractors are only capable of serving one such machine at a time is an indication of the real air movement and of

efficiency-loss through back-pressure from the filter system. Indeed, there is a definite limit to the air speed (and volume) attainable through vacuum pressure alone in a duct of any given size. An extractor which was *actually* pulling six hundred cubic feet of air through a 100 mm (4″) diameter duct every minute would have to move the air at over 7000 fpm – faster than is possible with a conventional, "low pressure" fan as used in mobile extractors, and especially so when the adverse effect of the filter is taken into account. Efficiency also suffers due to increased drag as the length of the ducting fitted is increased, and this factor must also be allowed for in determining the siting and power of an extractor in relation to the machines it will be required to serve. This is the reason that hoses supplied with mobile extractors are seldom more than 3–4 metres (12′) long × 100 mm (4″) section and proportionately longer as the section diameter increases. Smooth bore ducting (usually rigid) as fitted for permanent installations, reduces turbulence and drag and therefore allows longer duct lengths to be incorporated into a system of any given power without loss of efficiency.

age mobile extractor rated at 600 cfm can be used to draw waste from one high volume waste producing machine at a time through its standard 100–125 mm (4″–5″) flexible duct or, plumbed into a permanent system with smooth bore ducting and appropriate baffles (dampers) to pull from any one of several permanently sited machines. Large diameter plastic waste pipe is available from most builders' merchants and is very suitable for this purpose. Duct lengths should, however, always be kept to the minimum possible and long, vertical runs avoided. Assuming that motor power and fan size are unalterable factors in such a system, dramatic improvements in overall performance can, nevertheless, be achieved by attention to the filter arrangements as discussed in the following section.

Extraction Plant

For most production joinery shops and woodwork manufacturers at any level, the installation of a full extraction plant to handle every type of machine waste is essential. Although my advice is most certainly to have this done by a specialist firm who will *guarantee* that the system works, some of the factors influencing design will be of interest and help to smaller shops who wish to improve the performance of their own systems.

The starting point for every calculation is the speed of the air travelling through the duct where it joins the waste outlet of the machine it is serving. For chip extraction plant the optimum air speed is reckoned to be about 4000 fpm. For fine dust the speed is increased to around 4500 fpm. The size of the fan and motor and also the diameter of the main trunk of the ducting will be determined by the number and location of waste producing machines in the system and also, of course, by the total volume of waste which may be travelling through the plant at any one time.

The designer's objective will be to ensure that the air speed and volume movement at each inlet is suited to the particular machine and also that air speed is more or less constant throughout the ducts and not, simply, satisfactory at the machine outlets only. For example, if a single duct inlet (where it joins the extraction hood or canopy of the machine) of say 100 mm (4″) diameter and into which air is being drawn at 4000 fpm suddenly widens into an 200 mm (8″) diameter trunk, the air speed will drop to around 1000 fpm. This will be insufficient to lift the waste, and chips will accumulate, particularly in vertical sections of the ducting, to block the system.

Another factor, as previously mentioned, to be carefully considered by the engineer is the treatment of air after it has passed the fan but before it is allowed to escape from the pressurized side of the system. As in the case of mobile extractors, which have a comparatively small filter area, any undue restriction on the escape of air once it has dropped the waste it has carried results in back-pressure on the fan and a marked loss of efficiency. Obviously, in an industrial installation, performance must be consistent as any reduction in efficiency may result in a blockage of the intake ducts and the halting of production.

Knowing the total volume of air/waste that the system will be delivering, the engineer will calculate a filter surface area to allow for an escape of air through the filters at a rate of six to seven feet per minute. Remembering that air being drawn into the system was travelling at a rate of 4000 fpm (for chip waste), it can be understood that if the total filter area was the same as a cross section of the inlet duct area, air would be forced through the filters at the same speed (4000 fpm). Doubling the filter area halves the release speed as there is now twice the surface area through which air can escape. Doubling it again reduces the release speed of the air by a factor of four and so on. Following this principle, the actual filter area required to achieve a 6–7 fpm emission speed from a 600 cfm delivery is approximately 120 square feet. Fine dust extraction plant operates at a higher inlet duct speed again and, because of the increased tendency of floating dust particles to clog the filter mesh, an even lower emission speed of air through the filters is desirable – around four and a half to five feet per minute. The filter area for a similar capacity *dust* extractor would therefore be about 170 square feet. Compare these figures with the average fifteen to twenty square feet of filter surface in a 600 cfm mobile extractor and an idea of the room for improvement of this machine's performance can be gained.

Dust which accumulates on the inside of filters must be removed periodically (preferably at least at the end of every working shift) if the pressure inside the filters

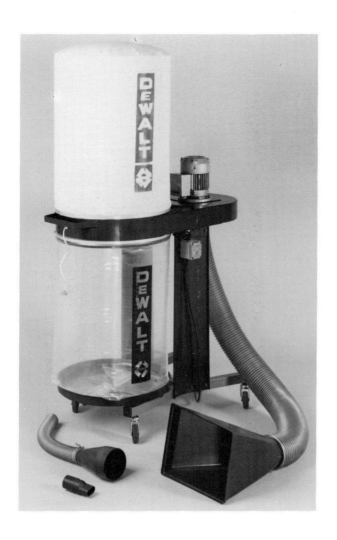

(DeWalt mobile unit)

Fig. 140(a) DeWalt's DW60 mobile extractor is typical of units suitable for extracting from most machines that will be used in small workshops, including those such as planers and spindle moulders which produce comparatively large volumes of chip waste. (In addition to extractors of similar performance both Startrite and Luna offer larger, mobile units which are suitable for connection to two or more machines simultaneously). (Photo: courtesy of Black & Decker Ltd.)

(Twin collection bag model)

(b) The filter surface area required for maximum efficiency is carefully calculated in every plant installation. This basic filter/collection module from U.K. Extraction Systems can be added to as the need arises. In its basic form (as illustrated) it is suitable for interior installation and the collection of chip waste only. The same unit can be enclosed in an explosion relief cabinet making it both weatherproof and suitable for fine dust collection. (Photo: courtesy U.K. Extraction Systems Ltd.

(6 collection bag installation)

(c) This plant serves eight production machines and is built on the module system described in figure (b). Including all the interior and exterior ducting, a return air system, automatic fire dampers and a 15 H.P. fan unit, the entire installation cost a little over £5000 at the time of writing. (Photo: courtesy U.K. Extraction Systems Ltd.)

(Enclosed metal cabinet)

(d) Any extractor sited inside a workshop and which is used for fine dust extraction must be enclosed in a metal cabinet which is itself vented to the outside atmosphere. This unit is specifically designed to pull waste from sanding machines and features a multi-leaved "envelope" filter providing up to 300 square feet of filter surface in a relatively confined space. A separate motor is built in for automatic filter cleaning.

141

is to be kept satisfactorily low. Three cleaning systems are commonly used. Firstly, manual, where the filter bags are either shaken by hand or a chain pull is attached to the frame which holds the filters upright allowing it to be shaken. Secondly, automatic shaking where a separate motor shakes the filter suspension frame and, lastly, by reverse air flow through the filters after shut-down of the plant. Automatic shaking is a feature of the best designs of true *dust* extractors such as the model shown in the photograph from U.K. Extraction Systems Ltd. The filter bags of mobile extractors should likewise be shaken from time to time with the machine switched off to prevent an excessive build-up of fine particles in the filter fabric which would similarly reduce its porosity.

Fires in extraction plants are frequently due to smouldering material being sucked into an inlet and being carried to the waste storage side of the system where there is a plentiful supply of combustible material and air. NO SMOKING is therefore a sensible rule to observe in all workshop areas. Other causes of fire or explosion are traceable to faulty insulation and motor fires where overload trips and fuses may have been short-circuited. Precautions to limit the spread of fires once started can be incorporated at the design stage of a system and one such is the inclusion of fire dampers in the extraction and return air ducts where they pass through the workshop wall to an outside waste collection point. These operate on a smoke sensing device which automatically seals off the duct as soon as smoke is detected.

Industrial extractors are removing potentially large volumes of warm air from the workshop environment and this brings its own problems as cold air is drawn in from outside the building to replace it. Such a continual loss of warm air would add considerably to the running costs of any workshop and, in a properly designed system, filtered air will be returned to the shop.

The larger systems illustrated in the photographs were designed and installed by U.K. Extraction Ltd., Unit 75, Wooburn Industrial Park, High Wycombe, Bucks. HP10 OTF. They offer the advantage to developing businesses that the installation can grow in line with future needs and without any loss of efficiency. For example, the filter module system can be added to, to cope with any conceivable input, as can the waste collection and storage facility. Also, the motor and fan assembly can be interchanged for a higher powered unit at minimal cost as the number of machines at work increases.

(Of interest to individual woodworkers and smaller businesses will be the information that U.K. Extraction Systems supply components for self-designed systems and items such as metal ducting, junctions, reducers etc. to any design, accoustic silencers, manual and automatic dampers (baffles), storage silos, fans, filters and so on are all obtainable separately in addition to their full manufacturing and installation service.)

Index